Dependent Origination

MAHAMEGHA

A Mahamegha Publication

Dependent Origination

Ven. Kiribathgoda Gnānānanda Thera

Published: June 2019

ISBN: 978-955-7940-01-4

Computer Typesetting by

Mahamevnawa Buddhist Monastery
Waduwawa, Yatigaloluwa, Polgahawela, Sri Lanka
Telephone: (+94) 37 224 4602
www.mahamevnawabm.org

Published by

Mahamegha Publishers

Waduwawa, Yatigaloluwa, Polgahawela, Sri Lanka
Telephone: (+94) 37 205 3300 | (+94) 76 825 5703
mahameghapublishers@gmail.com

Printed by

Tharanjee Prints

506, Highlevel Road, Nawinna, Maharagama, Sri Lanka.
Telephone: +94 11 2801308 | +94 11 5555265

My homage to thee—
Blessed One, the Buddha,
Great Compassionate One—
you who illuminated the entire world,
with your marvelous wisdom!

About the Author

Most Venerable Kiribathgoda Gnānānanda Thera is the founder of the Mahamevnawa Buddhist Monastic Order. He was born into a Catholic family in Sri Lanka in 1961, and at the age of six months his whole family embraced Buddhism. At the age of eighteen, he was ordained at Seruwila Mangala Raja Maha Vihara under the preceptorship of the Most Venerable Dambagasare Sumedhankara Mahā Thera, who was the Chief of the Sri Kalyaniwansa Nikāya and the Abbot of Seruwila Mangala Raja Maha Vihara at the time. After a traditional Sri Lankan monastic education, while studying for the Sinhala Honours Degree at Sri Jayawardhanapura University, he had the rare and unexpected opportunity to read the Buddha's discourses in the Pāli Canon, and as a result, he abandoned temple life and began to frequent forest monasteries and hermitages, offering his life to the Dhamma with a great desire to practice it.

Thereafter, having acquired a profound knowledge of the Dhamma by studying the Pāli Canon for a further ten years, Venerable Kiribathgoda Gnānānanda Thera accumulated manifold experiences in life while living in the Himalayas in India and the jungles of Sri Pāda in Sri Lanka. Venerable Kiribathgoda Gnānānanda Thera, by utilizing his experience gained over the course of many years in monastic life, began Mahamevnawa Buddhist Monastery in August 1999. While teaching the Dhamma and conducting Dhamma programs throughout various parts of Sri Lanka, he kindled in the people enormous faith in the Buddha's Dispensation. Venerable Kiribathgoda Gnānānanda Thera has authored over 300 books in Sinhala and several more in English on the Buddha's Teachings as recorded in the Pāli Canon, thus revealing the sacred word of the Buddha to the public. Those Dhamma books, along with CDs containing his inspiring Dhamma talks and Vandana verses, which explain the Buddha's discourses in simple Sinhala language, have elicited much praise from the people. Moreover, Venerable Kiribathgoda Gnānānanda Thera's translation of the Sutta Piṭaka into simple Sinhala language, helping it to be read and understood by people from any walk of life, is an unparalleled service to the Buddha's Dispensation—undertaken by the Venerable Thera out of compassion for the world. Teaching the Dhamma devoid of capricious personal opinions, by revealing only the pure word of the Buddha, is the unique quality of the Most Venerable Kiribathgoda Gnānānanda Thera's outstanding Dhamma service.

Mahamevnawa Buddhist Monastery

Mahamevnawa Buddhist Monastery is a center for the world-wide dissemination of Theravāda Buddhism. With the noble intention of creating an organization where the pure Teachings of the Buddha can be learned, practiced, and realized, the founder of the Mahamevnawa Monastic Order, the Most Venerable Kiribathgoda Gnānānanda Thera, established the first Mahamevnawa Buddhist Monastery on the 14th of August 1999, at Polgahawela, Sri Lanka.

Mahamevnawa Buddhist Monastery began with three simple huts—roofed with coconut thatch and polyethylene sheeting for walls—but has since become a vast Buddhist organization. Esteemed throughout Sri Lanka and the world, Mahamevnawa Buddhist Monastery has carried out extensive Dhamma service over the past two decades to spread the pure Teachings of the Buddha. The Dhamma service which began with a small group of pious devotees has since spread to the hearts of millions. A generation of youths searching for liberation have drawn toward Mahamevnawa, reigniting again the pride of the Gotama Buddha's Dispensation.

The Gotama Buddha's Dispensation was established on the island of Sri Lanka by Arahant Mahinda about 2,300 years ago at the Mahamevna Uyana in Anuradhapura. It was with the aim of spreading the sublime message of the Gotama Buddha throughout the world, that the name Mahamevnawa was given to this institution. "Monastery" is the English meaning of the Pāli word *ārāma*. Monastery and ārāma are words designating places where the virtuous and the righteous live. With the consideration of all these meanings, this institution is named "Mahamevnawa Buddhist Monastery." Mahamevnawa Buddhist Monastery is a warm and welcoming place for everyone to investigate true happiness through Dhamma and meditation. What makes Mahamevnawa unique is its effort to bring the Noble Dhamma to listeners in its original form. Here, the Buddha's Teachings are presented in modern language that is easy to understand, without compromising meaning for modernity. Mahamevnawa Buddhist Monasteries emphasize study and practice of the Dhamma according to the Buddha's Discourses in the Sutta Piṭaka. Further, the Mahamevnawa Monastic Order observes strict practice of the Monastic Discipline, practicing according to the *Vinaya*.

In Mahamevnawa Buddhist Monastery, more than 700 monks and 100 anāgārika nuns practice the Dhamma under the tutelage of Most Venerable Kiribathgoda Gnānānanda Thera. With over 60 monasteries in Sri Lanka, and 30 more overseas in countries such as Canada, the United States, Australia, the UK, Germany, France, Italy, Ireland, the Netherlands, the UAE, Cyprus, India, South Korea, and New Zealand, Mahamevnawa Buddhist Monastery continues to spread the Buddha's Teachings worldwide for the benefit of humankind.

Abbreviations and Notes

AN	Aṅguttara Nikāya
DN	Dīgha Nikāya
MN	Majjhima Nikāya
SN	Saṃyutta Nikāya
It	Itivuttaka
Skt	Sanskrit
Sn	Sutta Nipāta

All translations of Sutta excerpts were translated anew specifically for this volume from the Mahamevnawa Bodhiñāṇa Tripiṭaka Series, with consultation from the Pāli texts and existing English translations of the Sutta Piṭaka cited in the Bibliography.

For the reader's convenience, references to the Suttas (English titles and numbering) correspond to the respective English translations of the Sutta Piṭaka listed in the Bibliography. Pāli sutta titles are according to the Buddha Jayanti Sinhala-script Tipiṭaka. Sutta excerpts containing repetition patterns have been condensed by eliding the repeated phrases with ellipsis points. This practice follows that of the Sutta Piṭaka translations cited in the Bibliography as well as the Pāli Tipiṭaka itself.

Italicized text throughout the work refers to the Pāli.

Contents

	Introduction	xiii
1.	Making Intelligent Choices	1
2.	The Amazing Power of the Mind	35
3.	The Prerequisites for Wisdom	47
4.	The Buddha's Marvelous Realization	55
5.	Aging-and-Death	59
6.	Birth	69
7.	Bhava	79
8.	Clinging	93
9.	Craving	115
10.	Feeling	129
11.	Contact	145
12.	The Six Sense Bases	159
13.	Name-and-Form	169
14.	Consciousness	177
15.	Formations	187
16.	Ignorance	199
17.	Realization	203
18.	Cessation	213
19.	Essential Points to Keep in Mind	221
	Bibliography	242

Introduction

The Buddha was an Arahant who eradicated all mental defilements. He was completely free of greed, hatred, and delusion. The Dhamma realized by the Buddha was not taught to him by a god or a teacher. The Blessed One understood the truth of life through his own experience, effort, and wise consideration.

One usually gains understanding by applying one's intellect to knowledge acquired with external help. What happened in the case of the Buddha, however, was utterly different and marvelous. Such an amazing occurrence is unheard of since the life of the Buddha. Although the Taj Mahal, the Great Wall of China, and the Leaning Tower of Pisa may appear as wonders to ordinary people, in reality, there is nothing wonderful about them. Any number of similar structures may be built in the future through the blood, sweat, and tears of people. What wisdom or profound realization of life could one gain from gazing at these buildings? Absolutely none!

There is only one true wonder in the world; it is the wonder of how someone born as a human being achieved the highest state of Enlightenment without anyone's help, using only the power of his own mind. Only the Buddha was able to achieve this marvelous realization. The sublime Dhamma is not limited to unraveling the truth about the lives of human beings. The Buddha's teaching contains a clear and rational explanation of how the fate of all living beings, including devas, Brahmas, Māras, ghosts, animals, and those in the hells is determined.

His infinite wisdom and marvelous realization encompassed all phenomena and fields of knowledge. The Buddha did not develop methods of understanding the world through experiments using physical instruments. He acquired his knowledge in the laboratory of meditation using the instrument of his own finely tuned wisdom. The brightness of the sun's rays dispels darkness, yet the sun's brightness is limited. While one half of the earth is bathed in sunlight, the other half is in darkness. The inner workings of the mind cannot be observed with sunlight. The infinite wisdom of the Buddha, however, has no such limitations. His wisdom can instantly shine its light in any direction and its radiance far surpasses the brightness of the sun. The Buddha conquered the world with the power and light of this infinite wisdom.

What is this wonderful and infinite wisdom? What is this marvelous realization? We can find the answers in the gift the Blessed One bestowed upon us—the gift of the sublime Dhamma.

The great Emperor Asoka's son, Arahant Mahinda, brought the Buddha's Dhamma from India to Sri Lanka. Having ordained in India under Arahant Moggalīputtatissa and attained Arahantship the very same day he was ordained, within a short period of three years he was able to commit the Dhamma and the Discipline to memory precisely as taught by the Buddha and faithfully preserved by the great Arahants at the First Saṅgha Council. Arahant Mahinda did not arrive in Sri Lanka with limited knowledge of only a few passages of

Dhamma or with doubts about the Dhamma. By that time, he had achieved an unshakable confidence in the Dhamma along with a complete mastery of the Dhamma and Discipline.

He possessed virtue, concentration, wisdom, liberation, and the knowledge and vision of liberation. Arahant Mahinda thoroughly taught the Dhamma to the Sinhalese people in Sri Lanka. He ordained Sri Lankan lay disciples and taught the Dhamma and Discipline in the Pāli language. Arahant Mahinda only used the Sinhala language to explain the Dhamma and Discipline. These explanations are referred to as aṭṭhakathā, or commentaries.

Although stories and opinions originating from Sri Lanka were added to these commentaries, over time, they evolved independently without deviating from the original teachings of the Buddha. As time passed, the monks in India came to know about these commentaries written in Sinhala. A monk named venerable Buddhaghosa came from India to Sri Lanka to translate these commentaries from the Sinhala to the Pāli. He did not translate the Buddha's Discourses (*suttas*) from Sinhala to Pāli. It is evident that the Dhamma and Discipline existed in the Pāli language at that time, not in Sinhala. Venerable Buddhaghosa did not alter or translate the pure Dhamma and Discipline taught by the Buddha in Pāli in even in the slightest way. Unfortunately, uninformed lay people, as well as monks, erroneously claim that venerable Buddhaghosa altered the original teachings of the Buddha contained in the Dhamma and Discipline.

Nowadays, we see some lay people and monks alike haphazardly change, misinterpret, and distort the pure

Dhamma of the Buddha and its true meaning. This disrespectful treatment of the well-proclaimed Dhamma is a cause for serious concern. It is causing great harm to the longevity of the Buddha's pure teachings. Such deliberate distortions of the pure Dhamma will inevitably result in the disappearance of the path to Nibbāna. The corruption of the Dhamma gives rise to futile arguments. It leads to the growth of various factions led by unscrupulous individuals who arbitrarily distort the Dhamma for their own selfish gain and glory. Any unfortunate individual who willfully misrepresents the teachings of the Buddha is sure to be reborn in the plane of misery without even the slightest opportunity of hearing the pure Dhamma again.

We should beware that we do not commit such unwholesome deeds. As well, we must be careful not to take part in any such irresponsible activities that harm Gotama Buddha's pure teachings.

At times, we hear some strange opinions about the Dhamma being expressed by certain lay people and monks. For example, they make disparaging remarks about studying the Dhamma: "Why do we need to know so many discourses? Wouldn't it be sufficient to know just one discourse? In the time of the Buddha, they did not study as many suttas to realize the Dhamma." Sadly, this is a clear reflection of their lack of confidence in the Buddha, their inadequate knowledge of the Dhamma, and their distorted attitudes toward the pure words of the Buddha. Such individuals should be avoided at all costs.

The only solution to problem of endless suffering in saṃsāra is to learn and follow the original discourses of the

Gotama Buddha preserved in the Sutta Piṭaka in the Pāli language.

The pure teachings of the Buddha are well proclaimed (*svākkhāto*) from beginning to end. The excellent beginning of the Dhamma (*ādikalyāṇaṃ*) is virtue, or morality. The excellent middle (*majjhekalyāṇaṃ*) is concentration. The excellent end (*pariyosānakalyāṇaṃ*) is wisdom. The Dhamma consists of very pure meanings (*sātthaṃ*). It is explained in a crystal-clear manner (*sabyañjanaṃ*). It shows how to develop one's life all the way to the complete and utterly pure state of Arahantship (*kevalaparipuṇṇaṃ parisuddhaṃ brahmacariyaṃ abhivadanti*). These are the excellent qualities of the noble Dhamma.

We should not learn this Dhamma to waste time by engaging in arguments and debates. Our aim should be to understand the Dhamma and become free from mental and physical suffering. As well, our aim should be to understand the reality of life and achieve ultimate peace.

Consider the meaning of the following stanza on the Dhamma from the Jewel Discourse (*Ratana Sutta*), which Buddhists recite frequently:

Khayaṃ virāgaṃ amataṃ paṇītaṃ
yadajjhagā sakyamunī samāhito
na tena dhammena samatthi kiñci
idampi dhamme ratanaṃ paṇītaṃ
etena saccena suvatthi hotu.

The calm Sakyan sage found the undefiled
dispassionate, deathless, Nibbāna;
there is nothing equal to that state.

In the Dhamma there is this precious jewel.
By this truth, may there be well-being!

When we say, *buddhaṃ saraṇaṃ gacchāmi*, we take refuge in the Buddha who possessed nine incomparable qualities. These nine qualities are explained in the well-known verse *iti'pi so bhagavā arahaṃ...* It is shameful if one gives up refuge in the Perfectly Self-Enlightened One for the sake of gain and praise, marriage, or any other petty consideration. It would be like exchanging a precious ornament of gold, silver, and pearls for something worthless. Giving up refuge in the Buddha will not contribute to our well-being in any way. We should try to learn at least a little bit about the immeasurable virtues of the Buddha in whom we have taken refuge. We should recall these great qualities and rejoice in the good fortune we have gained.

When we say: *dhammaṃ saraṇaṃ gacchāmi*, we take refuge only in the original Dhamma taught by the Buddha. The six incomparable qualities of the Buddha's authentic Dhamma are explained in the well-known verse *svākkhāto bhagavatā dhammo...* Refuge in the Blessed One's well-proclaimed Dhamma excludes any reliance on distorted, false teachings being passed off as "Dhamma." We should seek refuge only in the sublime Dhamma consisting of virtue, concentration, and wisdom. We should put our complete trust in the profoundly clear Dhamma that eloquently explains the Noble Eightfold Path, the Four Noble Truths, kamma (Skt. *karma*), and Dependent Origination.

Similarly, when we say: *saṅghaṃ saraṇaṃ gacchāmi*, we take refuge in the community of noble disciples of the Buddha. The noble virtues of the Saṅgha are clearly explained in the well-known verse *supaṭipanno bhagavato sāvakasaṅgho...* The community of noble disciples comprises individuals who have attained the various stages along the path to Enlightenment—from stream-entry to Arahantship.

When we acquire a clear and thorough knowledge of the well-proclaimed Dhamma, it helps us to gradually eliminate our doubts regarding the Dhamma. Our confidence in the Dhamma will gradually stabilize and become steadfast. In this way, we as disciples will succeed in establishing a solid foundation in the Gotama Buddha's Dispensation. Then, we need not fear this life or the next. We can definitely experience joy and happiness in this very life itself, which also acts as a springboard to be reborn in a good destination after death. Rebirth in a good destination provides us an opportunity to hear the pure Dhamma again. We will then have the rare good fortune of progressing all the way to the supreme bliss of Nibbāna.

This book contains a minute fraction of the infinite knowledge of the Buddha. It describes in detail the Buddha's marvelous realization about the law of Dependent Origination (*paṭiccasamuppāda*). After realizing the truth about Dependent Origination, the Buddha taught us that the endless suffering in the cycle of birth and death is a result of the principle of cause and effect.

The path to Enlightenment according to the Dhamma is entirely dependent on one's own effort. Read this book carefully and remember well the vital points of Dhamma it contains. Strive hard to acquire wisdom and develop wise consideration. Realization of the Dhamma does not happen without effort!

Many monks helped and encouraged me in offering this book to you. May they too realize Nibbāna.

As well, may all those who contributed in many ways and rejoiced in this vital task of spreading the original teachings of the Buddha realize the Dhamma without delay!

May the blessings of the Triple Gem be with you!

Ven. Kiribathgoda Gnānānanda Thera
Mahamevnawa Buddhist Monastery
Polgahawela
Sri Lanka

Website: www.mahamevnawabm.org
Telephone: (+94) 037 2244602
Email: info@mahamevnawabm.org

Dependent Origination

Chapter 1

Making Intelligent Choices

You are bound to face many difficulties in life if you do not make intelligent choices. You may not be aware of this yet. Various political parties compete for your vote; you may already unwittingly be persuaded into purchasing goods and services produced by various companies and be the victim of various false beliefs and views. You face the challenge of making intelligent choices in the midst of all this noise and confusion.

Let us reflect on life for a moment. You go to school. You study and pass exams. You get a job and get married. You have children. You build a family. You eat, drink, and enjoy yourself. Little by little, you grow old. Illnesses arise. Eventually, you find yourself alone. Then, you die. Is this all there is to life?

In life there is always the possibility of associating with bad friends; any good person can be led astray by associating with bad friends. Once, an evil monk named Devadatta devised a devious plan to get the monks under his control. He formulated five disciplinary rules that seemed praiseworthy on a superficial level.

Devadatta asked the Buddha to make the following disciplinary rules compulsory for monks throughout their lives, with the devious intention of creating a schism among the monastic community: he requested that the Buddha make it compulsory for all monks to be vegetarian, survive on alms obtained solely on alms round, live under trees, use robes made from discarded rags, and dwell in the forest. The Blessed One did not agree to Devadatta's request.

Devadatta immediately approached the monks and told them that he was following these five strict rules of discipline. He invited those monks who desired to achieve liberation quickly to join him in adopting this supposedly fast-track path to Nibbāna. On the face of it, Devadatta appeared to be correct, even more so than the Buddha. Five hundred newly ordained monks were attracted to Devadatta's plan and fell into his trap. They left the Buddha and followed Devadatta with the hope of achieving liberation faster under his guidance. The all-knowing and infinitely compassionate Buddha was well aware of the great danger in associating with bad friends. He immediately summoned his chief disciples: Arahant Sāriputta and Arahant Moggallāna.

The Buddha sent his chief disciples to Gayā, saying: "Devadatta left for Gayā with five hundred newly ordained monks who have not properly understood the Dhamma. Go there quickly before any harm comes to them. Have compassion on them and save them." You may read a detailed account of Devadatta's attempt to create a schism in the Saṅgha in the *Mahāvagga* of the *Vinaya Piṭaka*.

The five hundred monks who were misled by Devadatta were extremely fortunate to be saved by the compassion of the Buddha and the noble Arahants Sāriputta and Moggallāna.

The Buddha and his chief disciples are not here now to save us from the clutches of bad friends; therefore, we must be extremely vigilant and intelligent in avoiding bad friends. It is particularly important to make an intelligent choice concerning your religious views and beliefs, as they could be one of the most powerful factors that affect your life. You may not be aware of how strongly the religious views you hold influence your ordinary life.

Facing the Problems of Life

Every one of us faces various financial problems in life. We often think that all of life's worries would be over if these problems were solved. Is this not why people make great sacrifices being separated from their family and friends to go abroad for employment? Many people undergo lives of severe hardship and toil without adequate food and shelter during these stints abroad. We can also see how some people are compelled to give up their culture and values for the sake of wealth and material gain. If we consider satisfying the five senses and enjoying ourselves to be the most important goals in life, it will not be possible to develop our minds and our intellectual capabilities. We do need money in life; it is reasonable to seek some pleasure; everyone aspires for a certain level of education and social status, but these are not the only important things in life. There are other things even more important.

This Is the Truth

No one belongs to a religion, language, nationality, or caste by birth. How could an infant who does not know anything beyond crying, smiling, and drinking milk practice a religion? At birth, it is impossible for an infant to speak a language or belong to any caste, tribe, or nation.

As the child grows up, adults introduce the child to all the things in their world, both good and bad. When the child starts speaking and walking by himself, he rapidly absorbs what he experiences. He learns everything gradually. Kindness or hostility toward humanity is developed afterward. The child's life is subsequently shaped by his association with friends, reading books, mass media such as TV, radio, and internet, education, and interaction with adults. The child develops according to the social framework established by adults.

With the passage of time, children develop a mindset of being segregated on the basis of nationality, caste, tribe, language, custom, or religion. They become exposed to discrimination and rivalries between various groups of people. As children reach adulthood, deep-rooted prejudices and biases have taken hold. This obstructs their ability to determine wisely what is true and what is not.

He who loses the ability to apply his wisdom and think independently is a helpless victim of the existing social system. He can easily be manipulated to achieve political or religious objectives. By then, he is a mere puppet. This happens to individuals who possess blind faith and lack the courage and ability to apply their own wisdom independently. If someone realizes this, he can direct his thinking with great compassion and love toward society.

Choose Wisely

If a religious teacher claims that his religion is formulated to provide benefit to humanity, one must investigate its historical truth. The texts of religious teachers should be studied impartially. We should investigate with wisdom. We should find out which religious teacher in history truly imparted wisdom, freedom, and peaceful living to the world.

We should ask who actually spread kindness and compassion among human beings. We should examine which spiritual teacher treated humanity with the highest respect. We should never accept anything with unquestioning blind faith. Fear, bias, and narrow dogmatism are the main components of blind faith. We should be vigilant to avoid falling into that kind of trap. We should have the ability to make the correct choice of a religion with intelligence, objectivity, and a clear sense of right and wrong.

We should free ourselves from a slavish mentality and select a religion that gives us the opportunity to develop our wisdom with an independent mind. We should select a spiritual leader who was pure and exemplary in his own life and in his teachings. The spiritual teacher we select should be a person who has achieved the highest level of perfection in human intelligence. Such a teacher should be a person who never compromised or deviated from his boundless compassion for any reason whatsoever. We are very fortunate to learn about a genuinely compassionate teacher possessing all of these incomparable qualities. What this great teacher did, spoke, and taught during his ministry spanning forty-five years has been well-recorded and preserved in the original discourses of the Pāli Canon.

The Marvelous Sage

At times, he walked alone. At times, he walked with thousands of disciples. He walked barefoot along dusty roads. He did not wish to be a burden to anyone. When his robe was old and frayed, he would go to the charnel grounds to gather cloth used to wrap corpses. The Blessed One washed, dyed, and made a robe from this discarded cloth.

The Buddha would go from house to house begging for alms. His hunger was satisfied by whatever was offered into his alms bowl. He spent the day with a bright and free mind. After attaining Nibbāna, sorrow, pain, desire, expectation, fear, anxiety, and doubt played no role in his life. Instead, the Blessed One's life was filled with serenity, joy, equanimity, rapture, the pleasure of solitude, compassion, and infinite wisdom.

This unique human being was born into a royal family of the Sakyan clan in the beautiful city of Kapilavatthu near the Himālayas in present-day Nepal. As the crown prince of this royal family, he was named Siddhārtha, which means in Sanskrit "the person who brings about goodness." As per family custom, he got married in his youth to the beautiful princess Yasodharā. By the time Siddhārtha reached the age of twenty-nine, he was given to serious contemplation and a curiosity to learn about the reality of life. The prince was overcome by a powerful and compassionate urge to find a solution to overcome the suffering of old age, sickness, and death. He was determined to find a solution for himself and all beings.

The Great Renunciation

Prince Siddhārtha firmly believed that it was possible to achieve true liberation of mind in this very life. He yearned for the day when he could leave everything and meditate in a secluded hermitage. The virtuous prince had to face many obstacles within the royal palace. But all the luxuries and bonds of royalty failed to imprison the prince. One night, he left the palace in search of the truth, like a bird fleeing its cage in search of freedom. On the day his son Rāhula was born, Prince Siddhārtha broke free from a mighty bond. He overcame a bond that a father would normally have incredible difficulty in overcoming. This incredible act of renunciation shows us the immeasurable strength of mind and determination that Prince Siddhārtha possessed.

For those who are obsessed by sensual desires in this twenty-first century, the renunciation of Prince Siddhārtha may appear to be an unpardonable act. However, how many mothers leave their infants behind to go abroad in search of employment even under challenging circumstances? How many fathers leave their families behind and endure great hardship in distant countries? There is no one to feel sorry for these individuals who undergo immense suffering just to feed their family. Some of these migrant workers do not even have the good fortune to enjoy the fruits of their labor.

Prince Siddhārtha, on the other hand, did not leave home to seek employment abroad. He did not go treasure-hunting in the jungle. He did not venture out to marvel at the beauty of nature by gazing at lush forests, cascading waterfalls, or exotic wild animals. The Bodhisatta did not set out to explore cosmic energy or to unravel the mysteries of science.

Explorers

Isaac Newton was a famous scientist who had an excellent intellectual capacity and a knack for investigative for thought. One day, while he was under a tree, he noticed an apple fall to the ground. Isaac Newton pondered why the apple fell instead of staying in the air. This incident helped him to formulate his Law of Gravitation. If he had not discovered the Law of Gravitation, he would have been considered a lunatic. No one else had considered the question that arose in Newton's mind. But the solution he found became useful to everyone.

Another well-known story is about how Archimedes discovered a method for calculating the volume of objects with an irregular shape. One day, while taking a bath, he discerned that the water level in the tub increased as he got in and realized the answer to his question. Archimedes was so excited that he ran through the streets naked crying out "Eureka!" meaning, "I have found it!" Such was his joy.

These two stories illustrate the joy felt by ordinary scientists when they discovered what they were looking for. The Buddha, however, carried out research that was infinitely superior and of greater benefit to devas and human beings in this life and beyond.

The Bodhisatta was the incomparable explorer of the human mind. He did not have the help of any teacher or religious textbook on his path to Nibbāna. He attained the highest level of concentration on his own. He refined his wisdom fully to understand the reality of life. We cannot even begin to imagine the happiness the Buddha felt when he achieved ultimate liberation at the foot of the sacred Bodhi Tree.

In Search of Ultimate Freedom

Siddhārtha set out with a single-minded determination to find a permanent solution to the suffering of human beings. He focused solely on liberating humanity from the helplessness and despair caused by aging, sickness, death, and the other problems of life.

Traditional Brahminism at that time taught that humanity experiences joy and suffering according to the will of a creator god. Brahmins were content to maintain their social supremacy by using such religious beliefs. They were also happy to continue the practice of various religious rituals out of blind faith.

Brahmins believed that their creator god could be appeased by animal sacrifice. Many thousands of animals were slaughtered, burnt, and the foul smell emanating from the charred flesh offered as a sacrifice to their deity. There were also occasions of human sacrifice to satisfy certain gods with an appetite for blood. Hence, these beliefs based on creator gods shackled the people's freedom of thought. Within these belief systems, it was easy for the Brahmin priests to control and manipulate the minds of people for their own gains.

When the Bodhisatta set out in search of the truth, various groups of independent, free-thinking ascetics had also begun their own journey searching for the truth. These groups completely rejected the existing beliefs of the Brahmins. They gathered around various religious teachers and started leading itinerant lives.

Siddhārtha Gautama (Pāli: *Siddhattha Gotama*) selected a similarly independent path and became a wandering ascetic. He wandered from one forest to another in search of a happiness that could be shared equally with all of humanity. He saw his fellow human beings struggling in a vast desert of pain and suffering. He resolved to deliver them to an oasis of relief, a true refuge.

The Bodhisatta had a clear goal and moved toward it like an arrow speeding toward its target. He possessed an extraordinary, unrelenting determination. His sharp intellect enabled him to grasp ideas rapidly without being misled by anyone. He was attracted to two well-known meditation teachers at the time—Āḷāra Kālāma and Uddaka Rāmaputta. The Bodhisatta stayed for some time at the hermitages of these two teachers and quickly mastered the full range of their knowledge. Realizing that he could not find the oasis, the refuge, he was searching for in these teachings, he moved on to persevere alone under the shade of trees and in caves. By now, the Bodhisatta had realized the futility of relying on the teachings of anyone else. He sensed that he was capable of finding the truth on his own.

This resolve to be self-reliant was neither random nor without foundation. The Bodhisatta had developed the necessary prerequisites to investigate the reality of life. He possessed a profoundly penetrative mind and an extraordinary intellect. He was fully equipped to explore and discover the truth by himself.

Ordinary Life

When the Bodhisatta was searching for the truth, the vast majority of people were not very different from people in the world today—they were generally not inclined to think deeply about life. The only goal in their lives was to live comfortably. Children went to a teacher's residence to obtain an education. Having grown up, men spent their days raising cattle and cultivating the land. Youth was a time for romancing. Women were content to adorn their bodies, raise children, and keep the hearths burning while the men toiled in the fields. Kings and nobles did their best to increase their wealth, while philanderers fought over women.

Though people adorned their bodies with the most elegant clothing, jewelry, and fragrances, their minds were filled with the same kinds of defilements we see in people's minds today. Their minds were obsessed by sensual desire, jealousy, hatred, vengeance, stubbornness, vainglory, fear, doubt, agitation, and helplessness. They were so preoccupied that freeing themselves from suffering and gaining peace and happiness did not occur to them, even as an afterthought.

While selfishness and conflict among people were the dominant features of society, only one person had the aim to end all suffering in order to bring permanent happiness to humanity. The Bodhisatta sacrificed a life of great luxury to meditate in forests and caves for this very reason. This rarest of human beings renounced his royal crown and became a wandering ascetic to achieve this goal.

The Great Sage Endowed with Wisdom

The Buddha knew that supernormal powers could be acquired by developing meditation to high levels, however, he did not approve of inspiring awe in people by displaying supernormal powers. Moreover, the Blessed One did not aim to coax people or deceive them with flattery.

Despite being blessed with extraordinary spiritual powers, the Buddha was always a compassionate friend of the everyman. The Blessed One was a kind and compassionate teacher who clearly understood the burning problem that afflicts human beings from all walks of life. He did not create any barriers or hindrances to deter people from approaching him and seeking solace. The Blessed One was always accessible and ready to help rescue human beings from suffering.

Extreme Self-Mortification in Search of Truth

While searching for the truth, the Bodhisatta subjected himself to a period of extremely torturous self-mortification and suffering. Certain ascetics in ancient India believed that food had an impact on the development of the mind. The Bodhisatta initially shared this view. As a result, he completely gave up eating delicious food and resorted to eating even the droppings of young suckling calves. Then, he increased the rigor of his self-torment by gradually reducing the amount of food he consumed. He reached a point where he ate only one mung bean for the entire day. In the end, he realized that severe austerity concerning food had no impact on mental purity. Thus, from his own experience, he abandoned the wrong view that mental purity can be obtained through food.

The Bodhisatta also held the view that mental purity could be attained by living in complete isolation in the jungle, hidden from the sight of others. He hid in stretches of the forest, and fled from thicket to thicket, just as a deer fleeing from even a shadow of a human. He thought: "Do not let them see me, do not let me see them." But fleeing in this way like a desperate deer and shunning all human contact did not bring him any closer to the truth he sought. Eventually, upon realizing that mental purity could not be attained by avoiding contact and speech with humans, he gave up the practice of self-isolation, having himself experienced its futility.

Then, the Bodhisatta experimented with various other methods of self-torment with the hope of gaining mental purity. He tried going naked, not bathing, plucking out hair, and not washing the dirt accumulated on his body. He gradually realized that these ascetic practices, too, had no relevance to purification of mind. After this understanding dawned upon him, as a result of his own experimentation, he gave up these practices as well.

Next, the Bodhisatta resorted to extreme physical torment of his body as he continued his search for truth. He spent extremely cold winter nights immersed in cold water. He lay down on the face of rocks scorched by the heat of the midday sun. In the end, he realized that this, too, bore no relevance to realization, and thus abandoned this practice through his own experience.

The Bodhisatta tried experimenting with controlling his in-breathing and out-breathing as he continued to torment his body in search of the truth. He practiced breathless meditation (*appāṇaka jhāna*) by holding his inhaled breath as long as possible without exhaling. While attempting to hold the inhaled breath trapped inside the lungs for hours, he felt excruciating pain, and his head felt as if it were going to explode. It felt as if the breath was trying to escape through his ears with a loud hissing sound. The unbearable pain in his stomach felt like his intestines were being carved out by a sharp knife. The Bodhisatta did not, however, succumb to this extremely painful ordeal. On many occasions, he collapsed and fell unconscious while practicing breathless meditation with incomparable effort. Then, after a while, he realized that tormenting the body with the idea of achieving mental purification is meaningless. Thus, he gave up on that rigorous endeavor after gaining an understanding of it futility through his own experience. At this point, the utter meaninglessness of self-mortification had become abundantly clear to him through his own experience.

Siddhārtha Gautama, the Bodhisatta, strived mightily to find the truth that had eluded everyone in the world. He did not have the help of any teacher or books to educate himself. He was the first person in recorded history to relentlessly pursue such a challenging goal. After six long years of struggle, he emerged victorious in the end!

One thing becomes obvious to us when we reflect on the life of the Buddha: the Blessed One had an unparalleled ability to consider everything wisely and investigate thoroughly. Because of his exceedingly penetrative mind, he succeeded in correctly discovering the path to true happiness and freedom.

Avoiding Extremes

The very first thing the Buddha understood was that life is dominated by the pursuit of sensual gratification. He saw the immense suffering and despair that arise when lives focused on sensual pleasures are interrupted by the harsh realities of sickness, aging, and death. He saw people desperately clinging to sensual pleasures until the last breath left their bodies, suffering immensely because they were unable to let go of their attachment to sensual pleasures. The Buddha understood well this obsession with sensual pleasures and renounced them having identified sensual indulgence as an extreme to be abandoned. He called this extreme "overindulgence in sensual pleasures" (*kāmasukhallikānuyoga*). The Buddha advised his disciples to avoid this extreme indulgence as something that is base, immature, common, ignoble, and unbeneficial. He did not utter these words out of any dislike for people who were obsessed with gratifying the five senses. Yet, it is because of people who are obsessed with gratifying the senses that all crime and misconduct occurs in the world.

In the palace, Prince Siddhārtha lived a life of great luxury, abundantly endowed with sensual pleasures. He gave up this extreme when he became a wandering ascetic only to fall into the other extreme of rigorously inflicting pain on oneself. The Buddha called this "the extreme of self-mortification" (*attakilamathānuyoga*). The Buddha gave up this extreme, having arrived at the definitive realization that it is painful, ignoble, unbeneficial, and does not lead to mental purity.

The Buddha is the first and only person in recorded history to directly experience these two extremes, reject them, and correctly identify the Middle Way.

The Magnificent Victory

The Perfectly Self-Enlightened Buddha succeeded in reaping the highest benefit of a human life by practicing the Middle Way that he discovered. He triumphed by overcoming all obstacles and reached the oasis of liberation. One can gain the eye of Dhamma, or vision of truth, by following the Middle Way of the Buddha. The Middle Way is the only way to acquire the wisdom of realization, overcome defilements, gain higher knowledge, and realize the truth. The Buddha declared definitively that the bliss of Nibbāna can be achieved by following the Middle Way.

He described this Middle Way as "The Noble Eightfold Path," consisting of the following eight components:

Right View (*sammā diṭṭhi*) – This refers to the knowledge of the Four Noble Truths. The noble truth of suffering must be realized. The noble truth of the origin of suffering must be eradicated. The noble truth of the cessation of suffering must be attained. The noble truth of the path leading to the cessation of suffering must be developed.

Right Intention (*sammā saṅkappa*) – Right intention is threefold: firstly, thoughts of separating oneself from objects of sensual pleasure—forms, sounds, odors, flavors, and tangibles—with the aim of realizing the truth (*nekkhamma saṅkappa*); secondly, thoughts of freeing oneself from ill will (*avyāpāda saṅkappa*); thirdly, thoughts of harmlessness based on nonviolence (*avihiṃsā saṅkappa*).

Right Speech (*sammā vācā*) – The Buddha divides right speech into four aspects: abstaining from false speech, abstaining from divisive speech, abstaining from harsh speech, and abstaining from idle chatter. Practicing right speech is necessary for one who is following the path of Dhamma. Right speech comprises words beneficial for both the speaker and others.

Right Action (*sammā kammanta*) – This means how one should conduct one's bodily actions; one should not kill living beings, steal, commit sexual misconduct, or use intoxicating drinks and drugs. A person who lives in this way acts for the benefit of himself and others.

Right Livelihood (*sammā ājīva*) – Right livelihood is concerned with ensuring that one earns a living in a righteous and blameless way, essentially leading life with a clear conscience, without causing harm or suffering to others. Right livelihood entails making a living without using coercion, deceit, trickery, or dishonesty.

Right Effort (*sammā vāyāma*) – This component of the Noble Eightfold Path constitutes great effort, diligence, and unflagging perseverance. The Buddha described four aspects of right effort: to prevent the arising of unwholesome states that have not yet arisen, to eradicate unwholesome states that have already arisen, to cultivate wholesome states that have not yet arisen, and to further develop wholesome states that have already arisen.

Right Mindfulness (*sammā sati*) – This refers to the cultivation and practice of the four establishments of mindfulness (*cattāro satipaṭṭhāna*): the body, feelings, the mind, and phenomena. The Buddha explains them in this way:

Mindfulness in contemplating the body

Mindfulness in contemplating pleasant, painful, and neutral feelings

Mindfulness in contemplating the mind

Mindfulness in contemplating phenomena: the five hindrances, the five aggregates of clinging, the six internal and external sense bases, the seven factors of enlightenment, and the Four Noble Truths

Right Concentration (*sammā samādhi*) – Right concentration is the unwavering focus on a wholesome state of mind, where the five hindrances have been subdued to yield a highly purified state of awareness. Through meditation, one can develop progressively more profound and heightened levels of concentration (*samādhi*) and maintain them at will. Right concentration includes four progressive states described as the first, second, third, and fourth jhānas.

The process toward the completion of the Noble Eightfold Path starts within the three aspects of virtue (*sīla*), concentration (*samādhi*), and wisdom (*paññā*). When virtue, concentration, and wisdom have developed fully, the mind becomes liberated. Someone who is liberated from suffering has a clear knowledge of realization.

Such knowledge is the insight arising from the knowledge and vision of liberation (*vimuttiñāṇadassana*). The Dhamma methodically explains how the gradual development of virtue, concentration, wisdom, and liberation culminate in the knowledge and vision of liberation.

The Bodhisatta, followed the Noble Eightfold Path to achieve the ultimate knowledge of liberation and thereby became the Buddha. This was the unmatched, unique triumph of the Blessed One. Then, the Buddha proclaimed to the entire world that he had become a Perfectly Self-Enlightened One (*sammāsambuddha*). This is a unique and marvelous occurrence that took place for the benefit of all of humanity, not only in the history of religion but in all of human history. The qualities of the Buddha fully encapsulated the collective goodness of the world and in the end, the unsurpassed Enlightenment of the Buddha sparked an intellectual revolution.

The Buddha's Kingdom

The Buddha's Kingdom is the enlightened realm that has been freed from the darkness of ignorance. Ramparts of virtue protect this kingdom. Its palaces are constructed from concentration and pinnacled with wisdom. These majestic structures continuously emit the rays of liberation. The Perfectly Self-Enlightened Buddha, the monarch of Dhamma, rules this kingdom. Venerable Arahant Sāriputta, the chief disciple of the Blessed One, is the Marshal of Dhamma in this kingdom.

Supreme Leadership

The Dhamma formed the basis for the Buddha's sovereignty in his kingdom. The Blessed One set the wheel of Dhamma in motion. Therefore, the Buddha's instructions are based on the wheel of Dhamma. The Buddha spent forty-five years as the peerless leader of the Kingdom of the Buddha.

Shortly before he passed away, the Buddha designated the Dhamma and Discipline, which he had taught and established over a long period, as the leader of the Buddha's Kingdom.

The Buddha is our spiritual king. Therefore, we lovingly call him the Blessed One. The Dhamma and Discipline, which he designated as the leader of the Kingdom of the Buddha, remain pure even today as preserved in the original discourses of the Pāli Canon.

People who are fortunate enough to recognize that Dhamma and Discipline, and practice the Noble Eightfold Path by developing virtue, concentration, and wisdom, can even today experience the wonder of the Dhamma as it was personified in the Buddha.

The leadership of the Kingdom of the Buddha is not an imperious leadership tainted by defilements. It is an absolutely pure leadership free of defilements. It is a leadership that transcends this world and heals the sufferings of life.

The Virtuous Sage

Siddhārtha Gautama, the Bodhisatta, gave up a life of luxury and adopted the life of an ascetic. His spiritual journey evolved and took shape gradually and systematically from that point onward. He developed his monastic life to the highest level by the sheer brilliance of his wisdom. This exalted human being directed his wisdom with great precision to achieve the goal of becoming the fully enlightened Buddha. He not only mastered his mind, but also systematically achieved total control over his sense faculties like a skilled driver in full control of his vehicle. It is truly amazing how the Buddha conducted himself regarding his bodily and verbal actions.

The Marvelous Words of the Buddha

The Buddha did not engage in idle chatter. He did not use humorous words to make people laugh for the sake of entertainment. He did not engage in useless talk. The Blessed One's words were utterly free of falsehood, divisive speech, obscenities, and offensive intent. So then, what did the Buddha's words contain?

Every word uttered by the Buddha conveyed an eternal truth and a timeless law. There is no one in this world with its devas, Māra, and Brahmas, ascetics and brahmins, its population of devas and humans who is capable of proving the words of the Buddha wrong.

If any person in this world, regardless of his or her religion, race, or caste, wants to learn of the timeless truth, it is only possible through the teachings of the Buddha. Because of the purity of each word uttered by the Buddha, we refer to his teachings as the noble Dhamma. His words have the power to dispel the darkness of ignorance and bring forth the light of wisdom. No one in the world can surpass the purity of the Blessed One's language. He attained this unmatched skill because of his perfectly virtuous speech.

The Buddha's Path Is Marvelous

The Blessed One's bodily movements were incredibly calm. His demeanor was serene. He did not glare or frown at anyone for any reason whatsoever. With his calm eyes, he looked at with equal compassion. When the Buddha attained Enlightenment under the sacred Bodhi Tree, he forever eradicated all latent defilements hidden in the inner recesses of his mind. Therefore, he did not wander in search of delicious food. He was content with whatever alms food he received. The Buddha's mind was not tainted in the slightest way by craving for food.

One morning, the Buddha woke up and surveyed the world with great compassion. He saw a fortunate individual worthy of understanding the Dhamma on that day. His name was Kasī Bhāradvāja. Kasī Bhāradvāja did not even dream that he would enter the path to understand the absolute truth of life on that particular day. He was only thinking of plowing his large field. Around lunchtime, the Buddha who was on his alms round came to where Kasī Bhāradvāja was working. Kasī

Bhāradvāja thought that he should tell the monk how to earn a living rather than begging for food. He started advising the Buddha. When the Blessed One replied to the farmer's advice, a discussion on the Dhamma took place. Impressed with what the Buddha said, Kasī Bhāradvāja took a bowl of milk-rice and offered to serve into the Buddha's alms bowl. But the Buddha had eradicated the desire for food and achieved control over hunger. It was not his practice to receive food in return for impressing others.

The Buddha uttered these wonderful words: "Dear friend, it is not our practice to consume meals obtained after reciting verses of Dhamma. Know that to be the nature of Buddhas." The Buddha spent the entire day happily, without any food. The Blessed One's effort was successful—Kasī Bhāradvāja gave up farming. He became a monk under the Buddha and attained Arahantship within a short period.

A Marvelous Form

The Buddha lived a perfectly pure spiritual life. Even the soles of his feet bore special markings symbolic of his pure life. The Kingdom of the Buddha is a community of pure and virtuous people. Its complete spiritual peace can only be attained through a pure life. There is no room in the Buddha's Kingdom for a person who leads an immoral life.

Monastic disciples of the Buddha vow to lead a celibate life when they enter monkhood: if this vow of celibacy is breached, then and there they lose their right to live in fellowship with the monastic community in the Kingdom of the Buddha.

Abundant Love

The Buddha led a life full of love and compassion, without any intention to harm the beings of the world. He did not approve of any type of violence. The Blessed One had extraordinary respect for human beings. He strongly disapproved of the division of human beings on the basis of nationality, caste, tribe, or language. The Buddha unequivocally declared that human beings should love one another.

He did not approve of any harm to human life. In the Kingdom of the Buddha it is an offense entailing expulsion for a monk with the higher ordination to intentionally support in the slightest manner even the destruction of a human embryo; if that human life is destroyed as a result of his actions, he loses his fellowship among the monastic community.

Protection for All

The Blessed One abhorred stealing. He trained his disciples to live without thoughts of stealing. He laid down a disciplinary rule prohibiting monks from eating anything that was not offered directly in to their hands.

The Buddha taught that people should be entitled to the security of their possessions, be it in a village or in the forest: one should not take anything that is not given. If a monk intentionally steals something of value, he instantly loses his status as a monk and severs himself irrevocably from the life of the Saṅgha.

No Room for Falsehood

The Buddha also strongly disapproved of people with fake virtue. He condemned false claims of higher spiritual attainment and deep levels of meditative absorption (*jhānas*) made with the expectation of receiving respect, fame, and material gain. He regarded such behavior as deceitful trickery and a despicable offense. A monk who falsely boasts and acts as if he has acquired certain levels of realization and psychic powers immediately loses his status as a monk. In this way, we can understand the high moral and ethical standards Buddha expected of his disciples.

The Buddha Opposed Intoxicants

The Blessed One considered the consumption of intoxicating drinks and drugs to be revolting. He expected lay disciples who sought refuge in him to abstain from taking intoxicants. Moreover, the Buddha instructed his disciples to refrain from selling intoxicants to others and making others use intoxicants. He understood the great damage caused to human life due to the consumption of intoxicants. The Buddha was so strongly opposed to the consumption of intoxicants because of his unlimited compassion toward humankind.

Work Tirelessly and Earn Righteously

Most people have to work hard to make a living, but some are tempted to earn money by fraud, trickery, and activities that cause harm and suffering for others. The Buddha unequivocally disapproved of this type of living under any circumstances. We are painfully aware of the colossal destruction and suffering caused by the weapons trade. Now we should understand more than ever before why the Buddha taught not to deal in weapons.

Further, the Buddha proclaimed that disciples who have sought refuge in his spiritual path should not deal in deadly poisons. In the past, Buddhist societies never used to utilize poisonous chemicals for agricultural purposes. Instead, water blessed by protective chanting (*paritta*) was used to drive insects away from paddy fields. This was the harmless method used by Buddhists who detested animal slaughter. Unfortunately, poisonous chemicals are now used to grow rice, vegetables, and fruit. As a result of our involvement in dealing with poisonous chemicals, we have now inherited an agricultural system that results in the destruction of small fish, insects, frogs, and worms.

Moreover, the Blessed One absolutely disapproved of the slaughter of animals. He taught that raising animals for slaughter and selling livestock for meat should not be done. The Buddha proclaimed that our compassion should also extend to the animal world.

The Buddha denounced trade in human beings, what is known today as human trafficking. He regarded slavery as a disgrace to humanity and declared that it should be avoided completely. Human trafficking still persists in the world because the value of human life is not appreciated.

Further, the Blessed One also disapproved of bribery, fraudulent transactions, price gouging, and cheating by using inaccurate weights and measures.

Effort Leads to Success

The Buddha walked along dust-covered roads to reach out to people in need of help. He endured rain, harsh cold, and scorching heat with immense patience and restraint. In this way, the Blessed One strived mightily to create a just society that valued humanity. As a result, during times when Buddhist society flourished, human beings and animals alike experienced great comfort. Trees and vegetation were nurtured. Rivers and streams were well protected. Lives were filled with comfort and happiness.

We hear about the so-called progress claimed to have been made by modern society in the last hundred years. But due to the inability to see the value of human life, our society has produced dangerous weapons with the power to wipe humanity off the face of the earth. Even the air we breathe is now polluted with toxic gases. The unscrupulous use of poisonous chemicals in agriculture has resulted in the gradual depletion of nutrients in the soil. Trees, shrubs, rivers, and streams are being contaminated. What will be the fate of a society that has not received the teachings of the immaculately virtuous sage?

Contrastingly, a society that has the refuge of the Blessed One's virtuous life will have the good fortune of living comfortably on this earth for a long time.

Even if one carries out the most exhaustive and objective search, one will not find anyone in this world of devas and humans with the immaculate virtue of the Buddha. Indeed, the Buddha possessed incomparably pure virtue.

The Sage with the Unshakable Mind

At first glance, it does not appear possible to discipline the mind. Therefore, almost everyone succumbs to the undisciplined mind and becomes puppets of the various feelings arising in the mind. They are deceived by the mind's illusions.

The Buddha led the solitary life of a monk. He did not relish the illusions of the mind. He practiced techniques to develop his mind during most of the day. Meditation was part of his daily life.

The Blessed One was skilled in directing his mind to a specific meditation object and maintaining that focus of mind. To be beneficial, the meditation object should be conducive toward developing serenity in the mind and assist in gaining realization of life.

It is possible for someone to direct his mind to ignoble, unwholesome objects and maintain that focus of mind. As a result, a dangerous one-pointedness of mind may exist. This state is called wrong mindfulness (*micchā sati*) and wrong concentration (*micchā samādhi*). It is not possible to achieve any benefit from this misguided state of mind. It only leads to restlessness and is not the path to purity.

Controlling the Illusory Mind

The Bodhisatta directed his mind using an extraordinary intellect. First, he identified mental weaknesses that were obstacles to conquering the mind and achieving serenity and peace.

Then, by using very methodical mental exercises, he eliminated those factors that were obstructing mental development. The Bodhisatta, gifted with great wisdom, discovered and explained the five main factors that block progress in meditation. He called them hindrances (*nīvaraṇa*). One who has the ability to concentrate the mind, can, with great effort get rid of these five hindrances and achieve a deep level of one-pointedness of mind (*citt'ekaggatā*). We should all be aware of the five factors that hinder the calming of the mind.

The Hindrances of the Mind

(1). **Sensual desire** (*kāmacchanda*) – The mind tends to repeatedly recall pleasant forms, sounds, odors, flavors, and tangibles to which the mind is attached. The mind has a desire to keep thinking of these sense objects that come to the mind. If one gives in to this desire, it is not possible to keep the mind focused on an object of meditation. Then, the desire in the mind for sense objects acts as a hindrance to meditation. This is called the hindrance of sensual desire.

(2). **Ill will** (*vyāpāda*) – It is unsettling when the mind recalls unpleasant forms, sounds, odors, flavors, and tangibles that give rise to anger and ill will. These unpleasant thoughts cause mental conflict. When the mind gets drawn into that conflict, it does not settle into a state conducive to meditation. Even if one begins to meditate, resentment comes bubbling up to the surface to disrupt the meditation. As a result, that anger alone can hinder one's meditation. This is called the hindrance of ill will.

(3). **Drowsiness and lethargy** (*thīna-middha*) – When one starts to meditate one realizes how difficult it is to focus the mind. This is because the mind is entangled with various activities in life through external objects. We usually do not feel any drowsiness or lethargy when we are laughing or talking. But as soon as we close our eyes to meditate, drowsiness and lethargy arise and we feel inclined to do something else. It is difficult to maintain effort, determination, and mindfulness when feelings of mental and physical lethargy set in. The Buddha taught that it is essential to overcome this weakness in order to conquer the mind. Because feelings of drowsiness and lethargy are barriers to the development of the mind, this is called the hindrance of drowsiness and lethargy.

(4). **Restlessness and remorse** (*uddhacca-kukkucca*) – Someone may not be hindered by drowsiness and lethargy, however, the moment one starts meditating, the mind wanders and scatters among various thoughts. This restless state of mind causes remorse when the mind is unable to focus on an object of meditation. Then the meditator experiences great disappointment and unhappiness. But one should not give up meditating under such circumstances: one must persevere and develop the mind to achieve a higher level of concentration. The remorse regarding the restless mind brings on even more mental anguish and unhappiness. This mental anguish leads to more agitation of the mind. This state of mind is described as the hindrance of restlessness and remorse. One must practice patience and equanimity to free the mind and overcome this hindrance. Persistence and relentless determination are necessary to develop concentration.

(5). **Doubt** (*vicikicchā*) – It is not possible to continue meditating when restlessness is present. At that time, if the meditator does not recognize his own weakness, doubts about the meditation enter his mind. Then, it becomes difficult to continually practice a particular meditation technique with confidence. This is the hindrance of doubt. There is a way to overcome this hindrance: one must learn the Dhamma well and develop confidence (*saddhā*) in the sublime Dhamma. When one completely overcomes doubt about the Dhamma, it is then possible to develop meditation.

The Blessed One stated that these five hindrances must be completely eradicated because they obstruct concentration and the ultimate realization of the truth. The Buddha discovered the existence of these hindrances that weaken wisdom entirely by himself. He also emphatically stated the need to overcome them. The Buddha was able to reveal these points of Dhamma only because he understood these hindrances well and overcame them himself to achieve the highest level of concentration.

The Tranquil Mind

It was easy for the Buddha to concentrate his mind. He achieved this instantly with the help of his innate qualities of supreme mindfulness, determination, and the ability to direct his mind with wisdom. The Blessed One was able to maintain his concentration in absolute stillness, like the still flame of a lamp untouched by wind.

The Blessed One discovered all the methods of meditation found in the Dhamma. These methods of meditation do not appear in any Vedic texts, *Upanishads*, or any other texts from or before the time of the Buddha. Even texts written after the life of the Buddha, such as the *Purāṇas*, the *Mahābhārata*, the *Rāmāyaṇa*, and the *Bhagavad Gita* include certain points taken from the Buddha's Dhamma. Hence, the authors themselves did not possess any realization of the points thus obtained.

Once, I visited a monastery of a disciple of Nigaṇṭha Nātaputta in India to see a friend. I asked the Jain disciple, who was naked, to explain something about the Jain doctrine. He started speaking about the Four Noble Truths and the Noble Eightfold Path. Apparently, he had studied these subjects under the impression that Nigaṇṭha Nātaputta had realized these truths. I was surprised to see how the Buddha's Dhamma had been incorporated into other religions. Nigaṇṭha Nātaputta did not even believe in the second jhāna.

Attaining Jhānas by Developing Concentration

The Buddha's knowledge of methods for taming the mind is unmatched. He was able to tame his mind and maintain a state of absolute concentration for any length of time. He could enter the first, second, third, and fourth jhānas, in that order. The Blessed One could also enter the fruition attainment of Arahantship (the unique meditative state of absorption achieved by an Arahant). He was easily able to stop breathing completely, to stop applied thoughts and sustained thoughts (*vitakka, vicāra*), to end all perceptions and feelings, enter the attainment of cessation (*nirodha samāpatti*) and remain in that state continuously for a week. The Buddha compassionately instructed his disciples on how to attain all of these experiences in exactly the same way.

The Blessed One possessed an incredible understanding of the different levels of concentration. He described the levels of concentration to be developed while maintaining the connection with the body as form jhānas (*rūpāvacara jhāna*). He discovered another type of jhāna called formless jhāna (*arūpāvacara jhāna*) that can be developed only at a mental level.

The Blessed One discovered a very advanced meditative state called the attainment of cessation (*nirodha samāpatti*) that can be attained only by extremely fortunate ones who have developed form and formless jhānas, and developed their wisdom up to the stage of a liberated one (*arahant*) or a non-returner (*anāgāmī*).

The Highest Level of Concentration

In particular, there is yet another level of concentration that the Buddha taught; it is called the fruition attainment of Arahantship. There are two main things that can be attained by realizing the Four Noble Truths, with the eradication of ignorance and the destruction of craving: they are true knowledge (*vijjā*) and liberation (*vimutti*). The attainment of true knowledge and liberation is also known as the concentration without interval (*ānantarika samādhi*).

The fruition attainment of Arahantship is not a state of mental absorption where there is no cognition or perception whatsoever. The fruition attainment of Arahantship is a mental state where it is understood through direct knowledge that all volitional formations (meritorious, demeritorious, and imperturbable) have ceased, all defiled kamma has ceased, craving has been eradicated, and lust, hatred, and delusion have been destroyed, and there is clear perception and experience of a peaceful and sublime bliss of concentration.

The Blessed One said that nothing in the world could be compared to the state of concentration (*samādhi*) in the fruition attainment of Arahantship. The Buddha succeeded in developing every possible level of concentration conducive to mental development.

Unshakable Concentration

One day, the Buddha was living in a small hut with a thatched roof beside a field in the village of Ātumā. Dark clouds gathered and it started raining heavily. The Blessed One concentrated his mind as usual and started meditating. Then, he reached a deep level of concentration. The rain intensified, accompanied by thunder and lightning.

Two brothers were plowing the field nearby the hut in which the Buddha was dwelling in meditation when the four oxen yoked to the plows were struck by lightning. The whole area shook with thunder but did not disturb the concentration of the Buddha even in the slightest way. The Blessed One was blissfully absorbed in meditation in the midst of the thunderstorm.

It is our incomparable teacher who was able to develop the mind to such a powerful level of concentration. It is the Buddha, the Perfectly Self-Enlightened One, who revealed the various levels of mental absorption to the world.

Chapter 2

The Amazing Power of the Mind

The Buddha, the incomparable sage, sacrificed everything in his life for the sake of liberation. He did not aspire to collect a large group of followers around him. The Blessed One's mind was fulfilled by concentration, wisdom, and liberation alone: he did not seek popularity, desirous of gain and honor.

The Miracle of Instruction

The Buddha taught the Dhamma solely out of compassion for the world. He encountered fortunate people who possessed the desire and ability to realize the Dhamma in this very life. He showed those fortunate people how to adopt the spiritual life he was leading. The Buddha's amazing skill in teaching the Dhamma was such that some were able to realize the Dhamma as and when they were listening to his discourses.

Before teaching the Dhamma, the Buddha thoroughly examined the mind of his listener. By doing so, the Blessed One was able to instantly understand each person's innate ability to realize the truth of life. He knew very well exactly what type of Dhamma to teach, and to which level of understanding the listener would develop his mind by listening to the discourse. Some monks came from faraway places to meet the Buddha. If the Blessed One determined those monks had the ability to develop their minds up to the level of Arahantship while seated right there, he would teach a discourse suited exactly for that purpose. At the end of the discourse, those fortunate monks would end the cycle of rebirth and be free from suffering.

This absolutely marvelous ability of the Buddha is called "the miracle of instruction." Throughout his life, the Blessed One dedicated himself to the spiritual development of any disciple who was genuinely interested in understanding the truth of life.

The Miracle of Psychic Powers

On one occasion, the Venerable Mahā Moggallāna, one of the Buddha's two chief disciples, was experiencing difficulties while practicing meditation alone at night. He started feeling drowsy during his meditation. Only the Buddha knew that the Venerable Mahā Moggallāna had the ability to develop his concentration to the highest level, attain Arahantship, and become the foremost among monks with psychic powers. That night, using his divine eye, the Buddha saw venerable Mahā Moggallāna dozing off while meditating. He quickly went there using his psychic powers and instructed the Venerable Mahā Moggallāna until he overcame the five hindrances completely and heightened his concentrated state of mind. In this way, the Buddha was fully attentive and committed to the spiritual development of his disciples.

Even at the time of his passing away, the Blessed One was utterly committed to the well-being of his disciples. The Buddha rested serenely amidst weeping devas and humans who had not understood the truth of life. At that time, a wandering ascetic named Subhadra rushed through the crowd toward the Buddha in an agitated state.

Anticipating that the Blessed One could be disturbed by the ascetic, the Buddha's chief attendant, the Venerable Ānanda, came forward to stop him. However, by that time the Buddha had already understood Subhadra's intentions. He said: "Ānanda, allow Subhadra to come. He has not come here just to ask any random question that comes to his mind. He is here with a genuine desire to learn the Dhamma." In the last moments of his life, the Blessed One calmly taught the Dhamma to Subhadra.

Great Compassion and a Wondrous Miracle

Once there arose in the mind of a Brahma, a higher heavenly being living in the Brahma world, the following view: "This life as a Brahma is permanent, this is everlasting, and this is eternal." The Brahma was of the view that he could keep the entire world under his control because he believed his existence to be indestructible and permanent. At that time, the Buddha was meditating under a sāla tree in the Subhaga Grove. He was contemplating how the lives of various beings are affected by the attitudes they held. The Blessed One observed with his mind the thoughts of this Brahma who was consumed by a view of permanence. Great compassion arose in the Buddha because he knew that the Brahma's view was harmful not only to the Brahma himself but to many others as well. He vanished instantly from where he was and appeared before the Brahma in the Brahma world.

On seeing the Buddha, the Brahma proudly exclaimed: "Come, good sir! I am living a permanent, deathless life. Your arrival here is most welcome."

The Buddha explained to the Brahma that he was holding a wrong view and that an immortal self does not exist in any world: "Brahma, previously you lived in a world called *Abhibhū*, and you were born here after having passed away from that life. The sheer longevity of your current lifespan has fooled you into thinking that you enjoy a permanent existence. There is absolutely no truth in that view."

On hearing these words, the Brahma felt offended. He decided that he should teach this stubborn ascetic a lesson. He challenged the Buddha, saying: "Very well sir. You are speaking without knowing my mental power. I shall vanish from your presence. Find me if you can."

The Buddha accepted the challenge: "Well, vanish from my presence if you can."

But amazingly, the Brahma, despite possessing such great power, could not move at all from his position. Just like a TV program being paused by a remote control, the Brahma's abilities were frozen at that moment by the immense power of the Buddha's mind.

Then, the Buddha said to the Brahma: "Well, dear Brahma, now I shall vanish from your presence. Find me if you can." The Brahma roared: "We shall see. I will not allow you to vanish from here." The Buddha vanished instantly and no one in the Brahma's assembly could see him. But he did not like to keep even the Brahmas in awe just by displaying psychic powers. The Buddha enabled the Brahmas to hear his voice and taught the Dhamma to them. He showed them the immaculate nature of a mind liberated from all defilements.

All Worlds Were Known to the Blessed One

The Buddha's amazing mental powers enabled him to maintain connections with all the worlds. Even devas and Brahmas accepted him as their spiritual teacher. When the Buddha taught his first discourse, the audience was not limited to the human world. Devas and Brahmas from twenty-two celestial worlds listened to the first discourse and attained stages of Enlightenment. There were no obstacles for those devas and Brahmas to become disciples of the Buddha. Listed below are the twenty-two worlds that listened to the first discourse of the Buddha:

(1). The Heavenly World associated with the Earth

(2). The Heavenly World of the Four Great Kings: *Cātummahārājika*

(3). The Heavenly World of the Thirty-three Divinities: *Tāvatiṃsa*

(4). The Heavenly World of Yāma: *Yāma*

(5). The Heavenly World of the Contented Divinities: *Tusita*

(6). The Heavenly World of those Divinities Delighting in Creation: *Nimmānarati*

(7). The Heavenly World of those Divinities Wielding Power over the Creation of Others: *Paranimmitavasavatti*

The Buddha taught us that the divine worlds mentioned above belong to the realm of sensual pleasures, or the sense realm. As well, he said that sensual pleasures are available in both the human world and these divine worlds.

The form realm and the formless realm are different from the sense realm. There is no pursuit of sensual pleasures in these realms. Only those who have suppressed the five hindrances and attained meditative absorptions with concentrated minds are born in these worlds. It is also possible to understand the Dhamma taught by the Buddha in the Brahma worlds listed below:

(8). The World of Brahma's Retinue: *Brahmapārisajja*

(9). The World of the Ministers of Brahma: *Brahmapurohita*

(10). The World of the Great Brahmas: *Mahābrahmā*

(11). The World of the High Divinities of Limited Radiance: *Parittābha*

(12). The World of the High Divinities of Unbounded Radiance: *Appamāṇābha*

(13). The World of the High Divinities of Streaming Radiance: *Ābhassara*

(14). The World of the High Divinities of Limited Beauty: *Parittasubha*

(15). The World of the High Divinities of Unbounded Beauty: *Appamāṇasubha*

(16). The World of the High Divinities of Refulgent Beauty: *Subhakiṇṇa*

(17). The World of the High Divinities of Great Fruit: *Vehapphala*

(18). The World of the High Divinities Steadfast: *Aviha*

(19). The World of the Untroubled High Divinities: *Atappa*

(20). The World of the Beautiful High Divinities: *Sudassa*

(21). The World of the Clear-sighted High Divinities: *Sudassi*

(22). The World of the Highest High Divinities: *Akaniṭṭhaka*

There Is No Mental Development in Modern Science

There are claims that scientific knowledge has resulted in unprecedented progress for human beings. But thus far, this knowledge has not enabled us to make contact with even one heavenly world. Contact with heavenly worlds is only possible through the power of a concentrated mind that has suppressed the five hindrances. Attempts at contacting heavenly worlds using any other method are pointless and unrealistic.

Now that the Buddha's Dhamma has spread to western countries as well, people in those countries may suppress the five hindrances and develop concentration based on the instructions in the Dhamma. They can succeed in attaining jhānas and gaining the ability to connect with heavenly worlds. Then, the world would inevitably be amazed by the extraordinary mental power of the Buddha.

Wisdom over Psychic Powers and Miracles

The Buddha, if he so wished, was capable of knowing instantly what anyone, anywhere spoke or thought. Feats of psychic power such as walking on water or conjuring up food were trivial matters that the Blessed One did not consider important. He knew that not everyone was capable of displaying psychic powers, and he also knew that it was possible to impress and amaze people that way. For this very reason, there were instances when the Buddha prohibited his disciples from displaying such powers. He used an interesting simile to describe the display of psychic powers: he ridiculed the act by likening it to a woman stripping off her clothes in front of a crowd for the sake of money. Rather than trying to encourage followers with blind faith, the Buddha wanted people to think wisely. As a result of the Blessed One's prudent decision, the immaculate Dhamma is still with us. If he had valued displays of psychic powers, we may have been left with only some magic tricks masquerading as the Dhamma.

The Blessed One's sole objective was to liberate beings from the endless cycle of rebirth. Therefore, he applied his concentration and wisdom to investigate all living beings in the world. The Buddha classified all beings that experience various kinds of happiness and suffering into nine groups. He referred to those groups as abodes of beings (*sattāvāsa*). They are shown below:

The Remarkable World of Living Beings

(1). Beings that are different in body and different in perception (*nānatta kāyā nānatta saññino*): they are human beings, certain devas, and beings in the lower realms (animals, ghosts, *asuras*, and hell-beings).

(2). Beings that are different in body but identical in perception (*nānatta kāyā ekatta saññino*): they are the beings of the first Brahma realm.

(3). Beings that are identical and body and different in perception (*ekatta kāyā nānatta saññino*): they are the beings of the ābhassara Brahma realm who radiate light.

(4). Beings that are identical in body and identical in perception (*ekatta kāyā ekatta saññī*): they are the lambent beings of the subhakiṇha Brahma realm.

(5). Beings that are without perception (*asaññino*): they are the beings of the impercipient (*asañña*) realm.

(6). Beings that, with the complete surmounting of perceptions of forms, with the passing away of perceptions of sensory impingement, with non-attention to perceptions of diversity, perceiving "space is infinite," inhabit the Base of the Infinity of Space (*ākāsānañcāyatana*).

(7). Beings that, by completely surmounting the base of the Infinity of Space, perceiving "consciousness is infinite," inhabit the Base of the Infinity of Consciousness (*viññānañcāyatana*).

(8). Beings that, by completely surmounting the base of the Infinity of Consciousness, perceiving "there is nothing," inhabit the Base of Nothingness (*ākiñcaññāyatana*).

(9). Beings that, by completely surmounting the base of Nothingness, inhabit the Base of Neither-Perception-Nor-Non-Perception (*nevasaññānāsaññāyatana*).

The Buddha was able to discover the existence of beings in these various forms because of the amazing strength of his mental powers; he realized definitively that all these types of existence are subject to impermanence. The Buddha was well aware of worlds with extreme pleasure as well as extreme suffering.

Planes of Misery

The Buddha taught us that there exists a world called hell (*niraya*) where countless beings experience immeasurable suffering. He also taught us that there are some worlds where beings suffer in complete darkness from birth to death.

According to the Buddha, there are also some beings who constantly experience thirst and hunger. This world is called the ghost world. Many ghosts survive on the waste matter oozing from human bodies, while some haunt human beings.

The Buddha has given an explicit description about the animal world as well. He explained how animals relentlessly attack each other and how the weak ultimately end up being the prey of the stronger species. The Blessed One referred to these lower realms full of suffering as the planes of misery (*apāya*).

One who is born inevitably dies one day. There is no one in the world who can avoid this predicament. However, this is not the only problem—the problem is being reborn again and again. One who is repeatedly reborn has to die again and again. The Buddha was able to understand this endless cycle of birth and death through his higher knowledge of seeing the passing away and reappearance of beings (*cutūpapātañāṇa*).

The Buddha's Panoramic View of the World

Someone who has climbed to the top of a mountain can look down and have a panoramic view of the surroundings far into the distance. He is able to see roads, houses, and people entering and leaving their houses. He can also see people walking in the streets. The Buddha's knowledge of the passing away and reappearance of beings is similar to this person's perspective from the top of a mountain. The Buddha realized the truth when he observed the world with this special knowledge. He realized that neither the world nor the beings in it were created by a god. Nor were they the creation of a devil. It was clear to him that the cycle of rebirth is a dilemma that exists due to ignorance about the true nature of life. When he realized this truth, great compassion arose in him toward the beings of world. Then, he directed his infinite wisdom to help beings permanently end their suffering. It is truly amazing how the Buddha used his wisdom toward this end. It is his great compassion that enabled him to fulfill his wisdom and achieve Enlightenment.

Upon achieving Enlightenment, the Blessed One liberated himself permanently from all defilements and delusions and became the most exalted individual, not only on the earth, but also in the entire universe. He began teaching the Dhamma, sharing his marvelous wisdom with us so that we may escape from the cycle of rebirth. That was his one and only goal.

Chapter 3

The Prerequisites for Wisdom

The Buddha taught the Dhamma solely for our sake. By the time of his parinibbāna, countless disciples had illuminated their lives through his marvelous wisdom. The Blessed One was extremely skillful in helping others realize the Dhamma in the same way that he had realized it. As a result, many of his disciples attained full Enlightenment themselves. We call these beings Arahants. Those Arahants, having reaped the full benefits of the Dhamma, had immense confidence in the Dhamma and treated it with utmost respect.

Genuine Disciples

After the passing away of the Buddha, the great Arahants led by Arahant Mahā Kassapa went straight to the city of Rājagaha for the purpose of safeguarding the teachings, the Dhamma and Discipline proclaimed by the Blessed One. Although there were plenty of means available at the time to write down the Dhamma, they considered it disrespectful to do so. They determined that the Dhamma should be held within one's heart.

After reciting the Dhamma and Discipline at the First Saṅgha Council (*saṅgāyana*), the great Arahants passed on to the next generation of pupils the monumental task of protecting the Dhamma from destruction. In Sri Lanka, Arahant Mahinda trained Sri Lankan monks using the same oral tradition. The monks were compelled to record the Dhamma in writing only under the most adverse circumstances when their own lives were at stake.

Acting with Foresight

For the first time in the world, the Dhamma was recorded in writing in Sri Lanka with the sole intention of protecting this rare treasure for future generations. It was a time of severe famine when monks did not have sufficient strength to commit the Dhamma to memory. With immense respect for the Dhamma, the noble monks came to coastal areas and committed the Dhamma to memory while surviving on the foliage of certain shrubs growing by the seaside. Their efforts were a resounding success, giving us the gift of the sublime Dhamma today. Although the Buddha is not physically alive among us today, we can feel his presence through his Dhamma. The path to Nibbāna is clearly recorded in the discourses. The Dhamma is alive and well in the fullness of the discourses. However, the biggest shortcoming we have today is that many people do not possess knowledge of the original words of the Buddha. As a result, they put forward their own views in place of the Dhamma. They describe the Dhamma according to their own preferred interpretations. This reveals their lack of respect and confidence in the Dhamma.

Some groups do not like others to obtain a clear understanding of the Dhamma. It is possible to manipulate society freely as long as ignorance of the Dhamma prevails. In contrast, it is not easy to mislead those who have a good knowledge of the original words of the Buddha recorded in the Pāli Canon. This is the why obstacles are placed to hinder the acquisition of Dhamma knowledge.

This Is the Moment

We still have some ability to understand the true nature of life. Therefore, we should not fall victim to the unfortunate fate of being misled by others. We are fortunate to have been born as human beings as a result of our past meritorious deeds; now we possess intelligence and the ability to think well and distinguish between truth and falsehood. Let us develop that mental ability as much as possible. This is called wise consideration (*yonisomanasikāra*), thinking in line with Dhamma. It is essential in understanding the Dhamma. Wise consideration means directing one's thinking for the purpose of realizing the Dhamma. The person who possesses this ability is like the tongue that is sensitive to the flavor of the food.

The Immaculate Dhamma

One who has the ability to think wisely needs to hear the Buddha's original discourses. These discourses contain clear words devoid of distorted meanings. When the meanings of words are distorted, the Dhamma becomes distorted as well. When the words in the Dhamma are not clearly interpreted, the Dhamma gets distorted. As a result, the distorted Dhamma leads to arguments and debates, instead of creating understanding.

The Buddha's Dhamma contains clear instructions for realizing the Four Noble Truths in this very life. The noble truth of suffering must be realized. The noble truth of the origin of suffering must be eradicated. The noble truth of the cessation of suffering must be attained. The noble truth of the way leading to the cessation of suffering must be developed. An understanding of these Four Noble Truths gives us right view. Right view does not occur spontaneously; two factors are needed to gain right view. One must get the opportunity to hear the Dhamma that describes the Four Noble Truths and one must develop wise consideration in line with the Dhamma.

The Dhamma and Wise Consideration

After hearing the Dhamma, one must engage in wise consideration, thinking in line with the Dhamma. The Dhamma that one listens to must clearly explain the Four Noble Truths.

We should rejoice over having the good fortune to study the Buddha's Dhamma, in its original form, even after twenty-six centuries. We should study this sublime Dhamma with immense respect and confidence. The Dhamma has the power to transform human life and bring complete liberation. We should study the Dhamma until we retain it well in our mind.

We should not seek refuge in our own intelligence. We should beware of people who distort the path to Nibbāna by saying that seeking refuge in the Buddha means seeking refuge in one's own intelligence. By saying this, they misinterpret the word of Buddha as their own knowledge. With this misunderstanding, one may reject the Buddha and disregard the guidance of the Blessed One. We should protect ourselves by listening only to the authentic Dhamma. Confidence arises when one studies the Dhamma with great respect and thinks: "Millions of people have achieved liberation through this noble Dhamma." Then the desire arises to retain the Dhamma in one's mind. When one tries to understand the Dhamma intelligently, it becomes clearer and clearer.

Begin with Confidence

When one tries to understand the Dhamma intelligently, a very powerful confidence arises in one's mind that the Buddha definitely achieved the exalted state of Enlightenment without anyone's help. One also develops a great admiration for the sublime Dhamma. As a result, great respect and admiration arises in one's mind for the disciples, the community of noble monks who have followed the Dhamma.

The fortunate person who acquires confidence with proper understanding in this way then develops a desire to follow the Noble Eightfold Path. Such a person is referred to in the Dhamma as the faith follower (*saddhānusārī*). The faith follower has faith foremost in his mind and rejects everything that is contrary to the Dhamma. He accepts only the authentic teachings of the Buddha. He gets established in Dhamma. His confidence is not mere blind faith. Blind faith has no place in the Dhamma taught by the Buddha. There is no room for truth within blind faith.

From Confidence to Wisdom

The confident disciple develops an investigative intellect through wise consideration, which is thinking in accordance with the Dhamma. He hears and learns about the sublime Dhamma containing the truth in the world—the Four Noble Truths. This disciple who directs his thinking for the purpose of understanding the Four Noble Truths is referred to as the Dhamma follower (*dhammānusāri*).

The Wise One Sees the Dhamma

The Dhamma follower gradually practices serenity (*samatha*) and insight (*vipassanā*) meditation to develop his wisdom toward realization of the Four Noble Truths. He is following the noble path to attain the fruit of stream-entry. He is called the disciple on the path to stream-entry (*sotāpatti phala saccikiriyāya paṭipanno*).

Right View

The first component of the Noble Eightfold Path is right view. The Buddha stated that the arising of right view in one's life is the dawning of understanding the truth of life. In the noble path, right view means knowledge of the Four Noble Truths. The disciple has knowledge that:

There exists a noble truth of suffering that must be realized.

There exists a noble truth of the origin of suffering that must be eradicated.

There exists a noble truth of the cessation of suffering that must be attained.

There exists a noble truth of the way leading to the cessation of suffering that must be developed.

This is the disciple's right view. With the arising of right view, self-view (*sakkāyadiṭṭhi*) is eliminated. Self-view is the deeply rooted view in the mind about the existence of a self over which one exercises control. All doubts about the Triple Gem (the Buddha, Dhamma, and Saṅgha) are eliminated. One abandons the mindset of wrongfully grasping behaviors and observances. An unshakable confidence in the Triple Gem is established. The disciple with right view maintains virtue (*sīla*) with proper understanding. He becomes a disciple who is firmly established in the Noble Eightfold Path. The spiritual faculties of confidence (*saddhā*), effort (*vīriya*), mindfulness (*sati*), concentration (*samādhi*), and wisdom (*paññā*) are established in his life.

The Buddha identified this disciple as the stream-enterer (*sotāpanna*), which means one who has entered the Noble Eightfold Path. From that point onward, the stream-enterer continually develops his mind until he realizes Nibbāna. He will never experience suffering again in the animal world, ghost world, asura world, or hell. Within seven lives at most, he will end his journey in the cycle of rebirth.

The Fortunate Disciple

The stream-enterer, who has firmly established his life in the path of the Buddha, is an extremely fortunate person. He is not a helpless, servile person who prays fearfully. He will not betray his faith and confidence for the sake of job, marriage, or livelihood. He will even risk his life to protect his confidence. The Buddha says the great earth will one day crumble to pieces and be destroyed and the great oceans will dry up, however, the confidence of the stream-enterer will not be shaken. His confidence is steadfast; it is immaculate, magnificent, and unflinching.

Please help everyone you know to acquire this noble confidence. Do not miss this precious opportunity in life.

Chapter 4

The Buddha's Marvelous Realization

We are living in the twenty-sixth century since the passing away of the Buddha. Today, we enjoy a great deal of material comforts and conveniences. All kinds of experiments are being conducted in laboratories. These experiments are resulting in strange and sometimes harmful discoveries. We have invented speedy vehicles to transport us between countries in a matter of hours. We are able to communicate instantly with any remote corner of the globe. We receive instant updates about what goes on around the world. Yet, we are unskilled and unsuccessful in establishing basic human qualities and values. Has this so-called progress solved the problems of humankind?

The Void Caused by the Absence of the Dhamma

The accumulation of lethal weapons is taking place at an unprecedented rate. Continued research and development is resulting in the invention of even more weapons that are detrimental to the survival of mankind. Intoxicating drinks and drugs capable of distorting the mind are distributed everywhere. Powerful nations exploit and pressure weaker nations and their people. Strange and deadly types of disease are spreading across the world. It is common to find books, films, and various technological innovations that distort sensual desires and lead to obsessions.

Ordinary, helpless people always fall prey to obsession with sensual pleasures, power struggles, violence, and terrorism. This is because scientists are unaware of the compassionate, serene Dhamma that looks at life realistically. A righteous leadership that sincerely embraces compassion and wisdom is nowhere in sight. Instead, we see malice, deceit, and flattery.

True Protection

The disciple who has found protection in the Buddha with proper understanding is a spiritually wealthy person. He has the good fortune to practice virtue, concentrate the mind, and develop wisdom. He is a brave individual who will achieve true contentment in life. A person does not become poor simply because he is lacking in food and drink. A person is truly poor if undeveloped in mind.

The Best Disciple

Once, the Buddha described the inspiring lives of Arahants who had fully realized the sublime Dhamma. He said that those noble disciples led an extremely simple life. Their possessions were limited to an alms bowl and three robes. There were days when they did not receive any alms food. At times, they would spend the night outdoors under a tree. Despite this, bliss, contentment, and serenity overflowed within them.

They had relatives who were wealthy in terms of money. Suppose those relatives were to invite an Arahant to their home and show him a pile of gold to match his height, a maiden of dazzling beauty, and a large palace saying: "Come back home and enjoy these luxuries. Give up your life of hardship." The Arahant would not even glance at the objects offered to him because of his deep understanding of the joy and suffering of life. Such a story can in fact be found in the *Raṭṭhapāla Sutta* of the Majjhima Nikāya.

Real Wealth

The disciple who has gone for refuge to the Buddha and has understood the true nature of life is not poor. Effort, courage, honesty, persistence, and mental strength are well-established in him. Therefore, he does not become victimized by evangelists of other religions. He does not suffer from any spiritual weakness. He is not misled by scientific discoveries. He constantly rejoices in the marvelous research and the amazing discovery of the Buddha, the teacher in whom he sought refuge.

The Buddha did not have any of the conveniences that exist in the world today. He lived alone and meditated in a hut in the jungle. His tool was an investigative intellect developed through extremely strong concentration. The Buddha was supremely skillful in being able to use his wisdom to discover the highest, purest liberation attainable in life.

With the successful completion of his research, he became a Perfectly Self-Enlightened Buddha, a *sammāsambuddha,* with immeasurable mental power.

The Righteous Objective

The Buddha was able to explain his method of research, which can truly be described as modern, to other intelligent people. He performed the noble duty of sharing his marvelous discovery not for a mere couple of years, but for a period of forty-five years. The objective of the Buddha's teaching was not to build a religious empire by collecting a powerful group of followers and destroying other religions and their adherents. His sole aim was to show people how to develop pure wisdom and how to use that wisdom to look objectively at the world. The Buddha's teaching aims at showing people how to use that wise perspective to become free from everything in the world. His teachings show the path to pure serenity through liberation. They teach us how to investigate methodically in a clear and simple manner.

Chapter 5

Aging-and-Death

The Complex Dilemma

First, the Buddha addressed the most sensitive problem that is also the most complex puzzle in life. He addressed this problem because people become utterly helpless and experience great sorrow when faced with it. This problem is death. Death is a crucial moment in one's life. It is an inescapable part of life from the moment of birth. Despite all attempts to cautiously avoid the process, all living beings gradually age until certain death arrives. Ordinary people's thoughts on death are usually limited to the great mental anguish and weeping that it brings. They do not contemplate anything beyond this sadness. Some describe death in ridiculous ways, saying, "God gave us life. Death occurs according to god's will. What is left for us to do is pray that the dead are called to god."

Only the Buddha came forward to tackle this complex problem of life and death and to find a solution. He sat under the Bodhi Tree in deep concentration, investigating the reality of life. In the first watch of that same night, the Buddha developed the first higher knowledge, the recollection of the past lives of beings. This knowledge helped him to clearly understand the long cycle of birth and death. Then, an extraordinary knowledge—the knowledge of the passing away and reappearance of beings according to their kamma—arose in him.

The Buddha's understanding of life was significantly broadened with the arising of these two higher knowledges. He realized that death is not limited to a single life. The Blessed One understood that death was inevitably linked with every birth. He realized that all living beings inherit death at the time of birth.

The Buddha's understanding of this reality formed the foundation for his immense compassion. The immeasurable compassion that arose in his heart motivated him to find a definite solution to the problem of death. He realized that this was the essential solution needed in life.

In Search of the Only Solution

> Alas! All beings in the world have fallen into misery. They are born, age, die, pass away, and are reborn again. Yet, they do not know the escape from this suffering. When will these beings discern an escape from this suffering of aging-and-death?
>
> SN 12.10 – Gotama the Great Sakyan Sage (Gotama Sutta)

Aging cannot be prevented through material comforts and conveniences, such as vehicles, health food and drinks, vitamins, and the medicine of our so-called advanced scientific world. The risk of death is in fact increasing rather than decreasing. There is no artificial method of avoiding death. We have no choice but to face this reality of life. The Buddha had a very clear understanding of this reality.

Short, indeed, is this life;
most die before a hundred years.
Barely does one live longer—
having aged and suffered, one dies.

Sn 804 – Old Age (Jarā Sutta)

Creationist religions avoid discussing the reality of life by teaching that only human beings are subject to aging-and-death and gods are immune to it. Only those who have faith in the god are supposed to be reborn in heaven and become immune to aging-and-death themselves. Those who hold these beliefs do not have the wisdom to understand that death inevitably exists wherever there is birth.

The Buddha states that even a god with a lifespan of an eon is subject to aging from the moment of birth. Therefore, aging-and-death is a universal reality that befalls all living beings.

The God Sakka Finds Refuge in the Buddha

On one occasion, Sakka, lord of the devas, came to meet the Buddha and listened to the sublime Dhamma taught with great compassion.

At the end of the discourse, the god Sakka became a stream-enterer. By that time, the god Sakka's lifespan was almost over. He passed away in the presence of the Buddha and was immediately reborn again as Sakka by spontaneous rebirth. By becoming a stream-enterer he achieved the protection and comfort of not being reborn in a bad destination. God Sakka was delighted with his fortunate rebirth and uttered the following stanza to the Buddha:

While staying right here, remaining in the godly form, my expended lifespan was once again renewed. Great sage, may you know it thus!

DN 21 – The Discourse on Sakka's Questions
(Sakkapañha Sutta)

No Crocodile Tears

We should understand aging exactly as the Buddha explained it. We should understand it wisely. One who does not have such an understanding of aging tends to get upset and alarmed at the mention of aging-and-death. He insults the sublime Dhamma saying: "Oh, Buddhism only talks about suffering. Why doesn't it talk about happiness?" That person does not have the ability to investigate wisely and understand the truth about life.

However, the Buddha did not teach that suffering is something to weep about. It would be extremely unfair to say, "Life is suffering. There is nothing we can do about it. So, just endure the suffering." Such a statement should be rejected.

Some political movements deceive the public by talking about suffering. They lament greatly in political forums that people are suffering immensely due to hunger. Politicians deceive the public with insincere words saying: "People are living in great misery due to the lack of food, housing, jobs, and good earnings. We will eliminate all these problems and create a wonderful world with abundant joy when we come to power." In this manner, politicians exploit the public by talking about suffering. The vulnerable public is deceived by their crocodile tears.

Some people do not have the intelligence to realize that they have been exploited for a long time by unscrupulous politicians who use the topic of suffering deceptively. Such people say Buddhism only talks about suffering. By making such statements, they insult the Dhamma that teaches the truth about suffering, the cause of suffering, the cessation of suffering, and the clear path leading to the cessation of suffering.

Their behavior shows that they do not have even the slightest knowledge of what the Buddha taught. However, an intelligent person with a genuine desire to understand the truth will realize that only the Buddha's Dhamma paves the way to realizing the truth. The Buddha teaches a universal truth, a timeless truth. This truth is a very delightful thing. An honest person finds the truth pleasing and falsehood repulsive. A dishonest person is averse to accepting the truth; he finds the truth bitter. The purest and most delightful truth is contained in the Four Noble Truths. It is an ever-relevant teaching that can be understood even today.

The Timeless Truth

The Buddha clearly explained the meaning of aging:

> Monks, what is known as aging? The aging of the various beings in the various realms of beings, their growing old, loss of teeth, graying of hair, wrinkling of skin, diminishing of lifespan, maturation of the faculties. This, monks, is called aging.

SN 12.2 – Analysis of Dependent Origination
(Vibhaṅga Sutta)

This passage describes an inevitable truth that we have to face in life. No one can honestly say this does not apply to him or her. The suffering of aging is a truth that is applicable to all living beings. It is a timeless truth that is not limited to a particular epoch. One who investigates wisely will be able to clearly see the truth that aging results in suffering, not happiness.

Aging-and-Death

Life goes through the process of aging and eventually ends in death. Those with minds steeped in ignorance think that death is a pleasant thing. Such a belief shows the extent of their ignorance. Some people would very much like to bid goodbye to their human life and die, thinking that death will give them the opportunity to meet their relatives in the next world. They will be able to break free from this wrong view when they learn the reality of life and death through the Dhamma. The Buddha taught that both birth and death fall under the first Noble Truth of Suffering, which must be realized. The Buddha knew very well that death is a sorrowful experience for all ordinary beings.

Ordinary beings beg for life when faced with death. They become utterly helpless. The Buddha described death as follows:

> Monks, what is known as death? The passing away of the various beings from the various realms of beings, their perishing, breakup, disappearance, mortality, death, completion of time, the breakup of the aggregates, abandonment of the body, severance of the life faculty:

this is called death. Thus, this aging and this death are together called aging-and-death.

SN 12.2 – Analysis of Dependent Origination
(Vibhaṅga Sutta)

"Self" Dies Too

All of us are living a life that will end in death. Therefore, we should understand this reality of life. If we constantly live our lives revolving around the concept of "mine," "my self," and "I am," we are destined to continue existing in this endless cycle of births and continue to experience the suffering of death. The Buddha's teachings are clear in the following verse:

Though a person conceives: "I am," "mine,"
the same he abandons at death.
The wise, being well aware of this,
never do they get attached, saying, "I am," and "mine."

Sn 806 – Old Age (Jarā Sutta)

Death becomes a critical, woeful, and terrifying experience for those who live immoral lives. However much one tries to hide or run away, there is no escape from death. At times, we face situations when life becomes unbearable. At such times, we think death would be a solution to end suffering. But when we are faced with death, we wish to be able to live at least a moment longer. We live here for a very brief period of time. Our life exists hand-in-hand with death. We can understand this only when we wisely consider the instructions of the Buddha.

All Is Subject to Death

Monks, all is subject to death. And what, monks, is the all that is subject to death? Monks, the eye is subject to death. Forms ... Eye-consciousness ... Eye-contact ... Whatever feeling arising from eye-contact—pleasant, painful, or neither-painful-nor-pleasant—that too is subject to death.

The ear ... The nose ... The tongue ... The body ... The mind ... Whatever feeling arising from mind-contact—pleasant, painful, or neither-painful-nor-pleasant—that too is subject to death.

Seeing thus, monks, the instructed noble disciple having realized the true nature of the eye, experiences revulsion toward the eye ... toward forms, toward eye-consciousness, toward eye-contact ... toward whatever feeling arising from eye-contact—pleasant, painful, or neither-painful-nor-pleasant ... He realizes with wisdom: "Destroyed is birth. The

spiritual life has been fulfilled. What had to be done to attain Nibbāna has been done. There is nothing more to be done to attain Nibbāna."

SN 35.36 – Subject to Death (Maraṇadhamma Sutta)

This universal law is applicable not only to the eye. It applies to the ear, nose, tongue, body, and mind, too. All the eyes, ears, noses, tongues, bodies, and minds in the world are subject to death. In the same way, all the forms, sounds, odors, flavors, tangibles, and mental phenomena in the world are subject to death. Similarly, all eye-contact, ear-contact, nose-contact, tongue-contact, body-contact, and mind-contact in the world are subject to death. Whatever feeling that arises from these six types of contact, whether pleasant, painful, or neither-painful-nor-pleasant, is subject to death.

Yet, ordinary beings wish that all these things that are subject to death would continue to exist without ever dying. This expectation itself also belongs to suffering.

Not Getting What One Wants

> And what, monks, is the suffering of not getting what one wants? For beings subject to birth there arises the wish: "Oh! If only we were not subject to birth! If only birth would not come to us!" Yet this is something that cannot be gotten by wishing. This too, is the suffering of not getting what one wants. For beings subject to aging ... subject to sickness ... subject to death ... subject to sorrow, lamentation, pain, grief, and despair, there comes the wish: "Oh! If only we were not subject to sorrow, lamentation, pain, grief, and despair! If only sorrow, lamentation, pain, grief, and despair would not come to us!" Yet this is something that cannot be gotten by wishing. This too, is the suffering of not getting what one wants.
>
> DN 22 – The Greater Discourse on the Foundations of Mindfulness (Mahāsatipaṭṭhāna Sutta)

Is This False?

Is it a falsehood to speak of the sorrow and despair that people face due to aging-and-death? All living beings inherit the reality of aging-and-death when they are born. This is certainly a sad fate. All those who fail to understand the reality of aging-and-death become utterly helpless. Those who believe in a powerful creator god pray for deliverance from aging-and-death. Others believe that aging-and-death occurs due to the influence of planetary movements. As a result, they make offerings and sacrifices in the hope of nullifying these supposed astrological effects and warding off aging-and-death. Others believe aging-and-death are natural occurrences. They claim that nature should be allowed to run its course without any intervention. Still others believe karma to be the sole cause of aging-and-death and that there is no possibility of countering the effects of karma.

Investigating the Cause of Aging-and-Death

The Buddha, the Blessed One with immeasurable wisdom, held an entirely different view regarding the cause of aging-and-death. First, he investigated the true nature of beings subject to aging-and-death. As a result, the Buddha understood that aging-and-death occurs due to impermanence. He realized that whenever something impermanent arises, it will age and die. The Buddha's wise investigation enabled him to find the permanent solution to aging-and-death.

Birth Is the Cause of Death

The Buddha realized thus:

> When there is birth, aging-and-death comes to be; aging-and-death has birth as its condition (*jāti paccayā jarāmaraṇaṃ*).
>
> SN 12.10 – Gotama the Great Sakyan Sage (Gotama Sutta)

Chapter 6

Birth

And what, monks, is birth? The birth of beings into the various realms of beings, their arising, descent into a mother's womb, birth, specific birth, the manifestation of the aggregates, the gaining of the sense bases. This, monks, is called birth.

SN 12.2 – Analysis of Dependent Origination (Vibhaṅga Sutta)

Hand-in-Hand with Suffering

The Buddha clearly stated that suffering arises along with birth:

Monks, if there is an arising, continuation, specific birth, and manifestation of form, that is the arising of suffering, the continuation of disease, the manifestation of aging-and-death. If there is an arising, continuation, specific birth, and manifestation of feeling … of perception … of volitional formations … of consciousness, that is the arising of suffering, the continuation of disease, the manifestation of aging-and-death.

SN 22.30 – Arising (Uppāda Sutta)

It is always something that is born and arisen that is subject to aging-and-death. Where there is no birth or arising, there is no aging-and-death. If there is birth, aging-and-death invariably exist. The Buddha realized this through wise consideration according to the Dhamma.

Is Birth a Chance Happening?

Birth is not an unexpected event that occurs by chance, nor is it an occurrence that can be set aside as a trivial matter. Birth is not merely the result of biological union of two living beings. It does not happen because of a soul being placed in a mother's womb by the will of a god. Birth is not a chance happening.

Birth is the tragic story of all living beings. Only the Buddha understood, through his infinite wisdom, that beings are born into this world in various ways. He stated that the birth of living beings takes place in four different ways. The Buddha used the term yoni, meaning the mode that generates a birth, to describe these four types of birth.

Birth Happens in Four Ways

> There are four ways in which beings are born: beings are born from an egg (*aṇḍaja*), beings are born from a womb (*jalābuja*), beings are born in a moist environment (*saṃsedaja*), and beings are born spontaneously (birth that does not fall into the former three categories is spontaneous birth, *opapātika*).
>
> DN 33 – The Discourse on Collected Points of the Dhamma (Saṅgīti Sutta)

(1). Birth from an egg – Beings that are formed inside an egg and hatch out. Beings such as chickens, birds, spiders, alligators, lizards, crocodiles, snakes, fish, etc. fall into this category.

(2). Birth from a womb – Beings that are formed as an embryo in a mother's womb and break out from the caul. Beings such as humans, cattle, goats, dogs, cats, pigs, donkeys, horses, elephants, lions, deer, etc. fall into this category.

(3). Birth in a moist environment – Beings that are formed in moisture, decayed flesh, or polluted water.

(4). Spontaneous birth – Spontaneously born beings are the beings that are not born from an egg, or from a womb, or in a moist environment. It is an instant rebirth of a fully-formed being according to kamma. Only a person who has gained the divine eye and has developed the knowledge of the passing away and reappearance of beings can see how spontaneous birth takes place. Spontaneous birth cannot be seen by means of scientific instruments invented by humans. Many questions arise about this kind of birth because it cannot be seen with our eyes. The Buddha stated that devas, ghosts, and hell-beings are born in this way. He also stated that some humans are also born spontaneously.

Wisdom Based on Confidence

One should understand the distinction between wise consideration in accordance with the Dhamma and fruitless arguments in the name of the Dhamma. Wise consideration is investigative intelligence that is based on confidence in the infinite wisdom of the Buddha. The sublime Dhamma was not proclaimed by an ordinary human; it was taught by an exemplary human being with comprehensive knowledge and wisdom, one who had attained to the exalted state of a Perfectly Self-Enlightened One. The Buddha was a sage whose knowledge was immaculate and complete in all respects. The Buddha explained many details to us about spontaneous birth in hell, heavenly worlds, and Brahma worlds.

Birth from a Womb

The Buddha explains how a being is conceived in a womb:

> Monks, conception takes place with the union of three things. Here, there should be bodily union of the mother and father, but still if the mother is not in season, and also a gandhabba has not arrived—then conception would not take place. Here, there should be bodily union of the mother and father, and the mother should be in season, but still if the gandhabba has not arrived—then conception would not take place. Monks, if there comes a time when there is bodily union of mother and father, and the mother is in season, and if a gandhabba arrives—then it is with the union of those three things that conception takes place.
>
> MN 38 – The Greater Discourse on the Destruction of Craving (Mahātaṇhāsankhaya Sutta)

Four Ways of Conception in a Mother's Womb

There are four ways in which conception takes place in a mother's womb:

(1). Venerable friends, some beings enter the mother's womb unaware, stay there unaware, and leave unaware.

(2). Some beings enter the mother's womb knowingly, but stay there unaware, and leave unaware.

(3). Some beings enter the mother's womb knowingly, stay there knowingly, but leave unaware.

(4). Some beings enter the mother's womb knowingly, stay there knowingly, and leave knowingly.

DN 33 – The Discourse on Collected Points of the Dhamma (Saṅgīti Sutta)

The birth of a being takes place due to the functioning of consciousness that is hindered by ignorance and fettered by craving. Only the Buddha realized that birth happens due to the connection between consciousness and name-and-form (*nāmarūpa*). He was able to unravel these mysteries because he understood the workings of consciousness. The Buddha explained how consciousness and name-and-form exist in a state of mutual interdependence.

Birth from a Mother's Womb

"Ānanda, if a consciousness were not to descend into the mother's womb, would name-and-form then take shape in the womb?"

"Certainly not, venerable sir."

"Ānanda, if a consciousness, after descending into the womb, were to depart, would name-and-form then bring about such an existence?"

"Certainly not, venerable sir."

In this case, the Buddha is referring to the death of the embryo in the mother's womb. There are situations when the embryo dies within one or two months in the womb. Sometimes an abortion is performed. Then, the delivery of a live infant does not take place because consciousness has left the womb.

> "Ānanda, if the consciousness of a young boy or girl were to be cut off in their tender years, would name-and-form then grow, develop, and mature?"
>
> "Certainly not, venerable sir."
>
> "Therefore, Ānanda, this is the cause, the context, the origin, and the condition for name-and-form, namely, consciousness."
>
> DN 15 – The Great Discourse on Causation (Mahānidāna Sutta)

The Interdependence of Consciousness and Name-and-Form

The Buddha taught that in the same way that consciousness supports name-and-form, name-and-form supports consciousness. He explained to venerable Ānanda how name-and-form supports consciousness thus:

> "Ānanda, if consciousness were not supported by name-and-form, would there be future birth, aging-and-death, and the whole mass of suffering?"
>
> "Certainly not, venerable sir."
>
> "Therefore, Ānanda, it is just this that is the cause, the

context, the origin, and the condition of consciousness, namely name-and-form."

DN 15 – The Great Discourse on Causation
(Mahānidāna Sutta)

This Alone Brings About Birth

By this alone, Ānanda, there comes birth, aging-and-death, passing away, and rebirth. By this alone, there comes designating beings by name, the use of language, the use of convention, and the use of wisdom. Just by this there is wandering on in saṃsāra. Just by this there is the coming about of life as it is experienced. That is, the mutually interdependent coexistence of name-and-form and consciousness.

DN 15 – The Great Discourse on Causation
(Mahānidāna Sutta)

Buddhas achieve their marvelous realization through noble research (*ariya pariyesana*). Discourses like the *Mahānidāna Sutta* give us a glimpse of how the Enlightened Ones achieved their realization. No other science in existence has been able to solve the mystery of how name-and-form and consciousness mutually cooperate to cause all the suffering of the endless cycle of rebirth. Learning the discourses of the Buddha allows us to understand the extent of the Blessed One's clear understanding and realization.

Consciousness Does Not Deviate

Consciousness turns back and stops. It does not deviate from name-and-form. By this alone, there is birth, aging-and-death, passing away, and rebirth—that is, with name-and-form as condition, consciousness comes to be; with consciousness as condition, name-and-form comes to be.

DN 14 – The Discourse on the Great Biographies of the Buddhas (Mahāpadāna Sutta)

An Unknown Journey

One thing becomes very clear when we investigate the Dhamma intelligently. Although the birth of an ordinary human being is a crucial event in saṃsāra, one is unaware of the underlying circumstances that caused the birth. One does not know that birth is the result of a chain of cause and effect.

Essential Knowledge

Monks, all is subject to birth. And what, monks, is the all that is subject to birth? Monks, the eye is subject to birth. Forms … Eye-consciousness … Eye-contact … Whatever feeling arising from eye-contact—pleasant, painful, or neither-painful-nor-pleasant—that too is subject to birth.

The ear … The nose … The tongue … The body … The mind … Whatever feeling arising from mind-contact—pleasant, painful, or neither-painful-nor-pleasant—that too is subject to birth.

Seeing thus, monks, the instructed noble disciple having realized the true nature of the eye experiences revulsion toward the eye … toward forms, toward eye-consciousness, toward eye-contact … toward whatever

> feeling arising from eye-contact—pleasant, painful, or neither-painful-nor-pleasant ... He realizes with wisdom: "Destroyed is birth. The spiritual life has been fulfilled. What had to be done to attain Nibbāna has been done. There is nothing more to be done to attain Nibbāna."
>
> SN 35.33 – Subject to Birth (Jātidhamma Sutta)

Now you know that there are four kinds of birth: from an egg, from a womb, from moisture, and spontaneous birth. Whatever types of reproduction there may be, they all fall within these four types of birth. A fifth type of birth does not exist.

Why Are Beings Born?

There are only two options for someone who believes that birth is the work of a creator god: either he is happy to be born and thanks the god he believes to have created him, or when he faces the endless suffering that follows birth—aging, sickness, sorrow, and death—he pleads to his god to help liberate him from suffering. A creationist philosophy can offer nothing more than offering thanks to and pleading for help from a god who is believed to be the creator of birth. One who believes that he or she is under the control of a god, and that god is always watching over him or her, can never understand the reality of life.

To believe that one was born according to one's own wishes, or that birth happened automatically, is to live for pleasure's sake alone. The purpose of life then is just to please the senses, to "eat, drink, and be merry."

A Way out of Delusion

The Buddha, without arriving at such immature conclusions, developed virtue, concentration, and wisdom to the highest level. This power enabled him to understand the reality of life. He did not investigate things with blind faith. The Blessed One started investigating independently using his own wisdom.

> When what exists does birth come to be? By what is birth conditioned?
>
> SN 12.10 – Gotama the Great Sakyan Sage (Gotama Sutta)

Chapter 7

Bhava

As a result of the skillful manner by which the Buddha employed his wisdom, he was able to understand the true cause of birth. He clearly understood with wisdom that birth is not created by a god, nor the result of one's own will, nor a non-causal phenomenon, but rather the result of specific causes.

> When there is existence (*bhava*), birth comes to be; birth has existence as its condition (*bhava paccayā jāti*).
>
> SN 12.10 – Gotama the Great Sakyan Sage (Gotama Sutta)

The greatest intellectual revolution in the history of mankind took place due to the Buddha's discovery. The Buddha discovered the most important factor needed to permanently solve the problem of all living beings. He found the permanent solution to cure the infinite sorrow and despair in the lives of beings.

The True Meaning of Bhava

We have now learned that birth takes place due to existence. The Buddha taught that birth ceases with the cessation of existence (*bhava nirodhā jāti nirodho*).

> When there is no existence, birth does not come to be; with the cessation of existence comes the cessation of birth.

SN 12.10 – Gotama the Great Sakyan Sage (Gotama Sutta)

So, it is clear that existence is not birth. Existence is the cause and birth is the effect. Many Dhamma books written recently translate *bhava* as "being," or "becoming," but these words do not adequately disclose the meaning of the Pāli word bhava; they are mere placeholders. It is inadequate to translate bhava as "being," or "becoming," when in the teachings of the Buddha the meaning of the word bhava is clearly defined. The Book of the Threes in the Numerical Discourses of the Buddha (Aṅguttara Nikāya) contains a discourse that clearly explains the meaning of the word bhava as "the arranging of kamma to bear fruit."

Here Is the Truth

One day, the Venerable Ānanda approached the Buddha and asked:

> "Venerable sir, it is said: 'bhava, bhava.' Based on what, Venerable sir, is there bhava?"

The Buddha replied to the Venerable Ānanda's question with a very clear explanation:

> "If Ānanda, there were no kamma to bear fruit relevant to the sensory element (realm), then would there be established such a thing as sense-sphere existence (*kāma bhava*)?"

> "No, venerable sir."

"In this way, Ānanda, kamma is the field, consciousness is the seed, and craving is the water. For beings enveloped by ignorance and fettered by craving, their volition and aspiration are established in the inferior element (*hīna dhātu*). In this way there is the production of renewed existence in the future."

AN 3.77 – Volition and Aspiration (Dutiya Bhava Sutta)

Here, the Buddha refers to the sensory realm as the "inferior element."

Three Types of Kammic Arrangement (Bhava)

The Buddha identified three types of kammic arrangement:

And what, monks, is bhava? There are these three kinds of bhava: the arranging of kamma to bear fruit in the sense sphere (*kāma bhava*), the arranging of kamma to bear fruit in the form sphere (*rūpa bhava*), and the arranging of kamma to bear fruit in the formless sphere (*arūpa bhava*). This, monks, is called bhava.

SN 12.2 – Analysis of Dependent Origination
(Vibhaṅga Sutta)

In the above discourse describing bhava, the *Dutiya Bhava Sutta*, the Buddha refers to the sensory realm as the inferior element, the form realm as the middling element, and the formless realm as the superior element. When describing all three types of bhava, he referred to kamma as the field, consciousness as the seed which grows, and craving as the water.

Understand the Arising of Bhava

One thing is very clear to us: bhava ceases to be if there is no arranging of kamma to bear fruit in the sensory, form, or formless realms. And if bhava ceases, there would be no birth. If bhava is present, then definitely there shall be birth.

Once, the Venerable Mahā Koṭṭhita went to the Venerable Sāriputta and said:

(Question) "Venerable friend, how does the arranging of kamma to bear fruit in the future once again bring about birth?"

The Venerable Sāriputta gave him a very clear reply:

(Answer) "Venerable friend, for beings hindered by ignorance and fettered by craving, delighting in whatever they experience, future birth comes to be once again with the arranging of kamma to bear fruit in the future."

MN 43 – The Greater Series of Questions and Answers (Mahāvedalla Sutta)

The Cessation of Bhava

Then, the Venerable Mahā Koṭṭhita asked the Venerable Sāriputta:

(Question) "Venerable friend, how does the absence of the arranging of kamma to bear fruit in the future not bring about birth?"

(Answer) "Venerable friend, with the elimination of attachment toward ignorance, with the arising of true

> knowledge, and with the cessation of craving, the absence of the arranging of kamma to bear fruit in the future does not bring about birth."
>
> MN 43 – The Greater Series of Questions and Answers (Mahāvedalla Sutta)

One thing must be clear to us now—bhava is not birth. It is the cause of birth. We are now in the human world. The human world belongs to the sense sphere. The sense sphere is where kamma bears fruit for beings to experience pleasure and pain through the sense objects of forms, sounds, odors, flavors, and tangibles.

At the time of death in our previous life, kamma had been arranged to bear fruit in the sense sphere. As a result, we were born in the sense sphere so that we may experience the results of kamma arranged to be experienced in the sense sphere. Therefore, kamma, or intentional actions, exclusively influence birth. Only a person who succeeds in achieving the cessation of all kamma will be liberated from rebirth.

The Significance of Kamma

One day, a Brahmin student named Subha asked the Buddha what causes various beings to be superior or inferior. Subha wanted to know why beings are short-lived and long-lived, sickly and healthy, ugly and beautiful, uninfluential and influential, poor and wealthy, low-born and high-born, and unintelligent and wise. The Blessed One replied:

> Young man, beings exist as owners of their kamma, heirs to their kamma; with kamma as their birthplace, with kamma as their relatives, with kamma as their

refuge. It is kamma that differentiates beings as inferior and superior.

MN 135 – The Shorter Exposition of Action
(Cūḷakammavibhaṅga Sutta)

Interim Bhava?

Therefore, bhava means the arranging of kamma to bear fruit. Those who have not understood bhava in this way speak of an interim bhava, a gap between two states of existence, considering it to be a bhava that is neither *kāmabhava*, *rūpabhava*, nor *arūpabhava*. They arrive at the above conclusions because they have misunderstood bhava as birth in a mother's womb.

Suppose a person dies, and he has not yet been conceived in a mother's womb, then in the meantime (between death and conception) he should exist somewhere. Hence, from the moment of death until rebirth in a mother's womb, for a certain period of time he dwells in a state of existence; this is misinterpreted as an interim bhava.

Once, a wanderer named Vacchagotta questioned the Buddha on a similar matter:

"Master Gotama, when a being has abandoned this body but has not yet taken up another body, what does Master Gotama declare to be its fuel?"

"When, Vaccha, a being has abandoned this body but has not yet taken up another body, I declare that it is fueled by craving. For that duration, craving is its fuel."

SN 44.9 – The Debating Hall (Kutūhalasālā Sutta)

The Buddha, too, accepted that there is an interval between death and being reborn in a mother's womb. However, this is just a gap between death and rebirth, not an interim bhava. A state of spontaneous birth (*opapātika*) exists in the time span between death and rebirth in a mother's womb. Craving and clinging are present in this temporary state of existence. Where there is clinging, the arranging of kamma to bear fruit (i.e., bhava) is always present. And where bhava is present, birth is always the natural result. The law of Dependent Origination always holds true. This law applies, without exception, to all beings with defilements.

The belief that all beings who die remain in an interim state before entering a mother's womb is an utter falsehood. It is a belief that is not in line with the Dhamma. All beings that die do not enter a temporary state of spontaneous rebirth until they take rebirth in the next life. There are several discourses by the Buddha on this topic in the chapter of the Noble Truths (Saccasaṃyutta) in the Connected Discourses of the Buddha (Saṃyutta Nikāya).

Recognize the Dhamma

Once, the Buddha took up a little bit of soil in his fingernail and asked the monks:

> "Monks, what do you think, which is more: the little bit of soil that I have taken up in the tip of my fingernail or the soil of the great earth?"
>
> "Venerable sir, the soil of the great earth is more. The little bit of soil that the Blessed One has taken up in the tip of his fingernail is trifling. Compared to the great

earth, the little bit of soil that the Blessed One has taken up in his fingernail is not calculable, does not bear comparison, does not amount even to a fraction."

"Monks, in the same way, the number of humans who die and are reborn as humans or devas is very few, like the little bit of soil in the tip of my fingernail. The vast majority of humans who die, similar to the soil of the great earth, are reborn in hell, the animal world, or the ghost world..."

SN 56.102-107 – Passing Away As Humans
(Manussacuti Suttas)

Now that we know that bhava means the arranging of kamma to bear fruit, it is clear that kamma is not a trivial matter. However, this does not mean that kamma is permanent; kamma is impermanent, it is a thing conditioned of causes, and therefore ceases when the causes cease. The complete destruction of kamma results in the attainment of liberation, becoming an Arahant.

What Is Kamma?

We should understand kamma as something that accrues to yield results. The Buddha gave a very clear description of kamma:

"It is volition, monks, that I call kamma.
(*Cetanāhaṃ, bhikkhave, kammaṃ vadāmi*).
For having willed, one acts by body, speech, or mind.
(*Cetayitvā kammaṃ karoti—kāyena vācāya manasā*)."

AN 6.63 – Penetrative (Nibbedhika Sutta)

The Buddha explained that there are six classes of volition:

> Monks, what are volitional formations (*saṅkhārā*)? There are these six classes of volition: volition regarding forms, volition regarding sounds, volition regarding odors, volition regarding flavors, volition regarding tangibles, and volition regarding mental phenomena.
>
> SN 22.57 – The Seven Cases (Sattaṭṭhāna Sutta)

Therefore, volition arises regarding forms, sounds, odors, flavors, tangibles, and mental phenomena. What is the cause of volition, or kamma?

Kamma Is Also a Conditioned Thing

> Monks, what is the arising of the basis for kamma? Monks, contact is the arising of the basis for kamma.
>
> AN 6.63 – Penetrative (Nibbedhika Sutta)

Contact is the union of three things. There are six types of contact that occur in the sense bases: they are eye-contact, ear-contact, nose-contact, tongue-contact, body-contact, and mind-contact. Eye-contact is the union of the eye, forms, and eye-consciousness; ear-contact is the union of the ear, sounds, and ear-consciousness; nose-contact is the union of the nose, odors, and nose-consciousness; tongue-contact is the union of the tongue, flavors, and tongue-consciousness; body-contact is the union of the body, tangibles, and body-consciousness; mind-contact is the union of the mind, mental phenomena, and mind-consciousness. In this way, the union of three things is contact, and with contact as condition, feeling, perception, and volition arise.

The Nature of Kamma

Kamma operates in inexplicable ways. The Buddha stated that the scope of the results of kamma (*kammavipāka*) is so complex that it is beyond comprehension of the mind. However, the accrual of kamma is something that can be stopped, as kamma too is impermanent and subject to cessation.

The Buddha explained that we must consider kamma as a field, consciousness as the seed that grows in the field of kamma and craving as the water that helps the seed of consciousness to grow.

The Buddha described very clearly how the seed of consciousness grows in the field of kamma:

> Monks, if a person immersed in ignorance accrues a meritorious volitional formation (good kamma), his consciousness is formed based on that merit. If he accrues a demeritorious volitional formation (bad kamma), his consciousness is formed based on that demerit. If he accrues an imperturbable volitional formation (kamma accrued when dwelling in form and formless jhāna states), his consciousness is formed based on that imperturbable volitional formation.
>
> SN 12.51 – Thorough Investigation (Parivīmaṃsana Sutta)

Suffering Grows

How does a plant grow in the earth? First, the seedling's roots push down into the earth. Then, the roots absorb water and nutrients from the earth and grow. The Buddha explained that the operation of consciousness is similar to the growth of a seedling.

> Monks, the four stations of consciousness (form, feeling, perception, and volitional formations) should be realized as like the earth. Monks, delight and lust should be realized as like water. Monks, consciousness supported by nutriment should be realized as like the five kinds of seeds.
>
> Consciousness, monks, if it exists, exists immersed in form, focused on form, based upon form, being moistened by delight and lust—then consciousness grows, develops, and matures. Consciousness, monks, if it exists, exists immersed in feeling ... Consciousness, monks, if it exists, exists immersed in perception ... Consciousness, monks, if it exists, exists immersed in volitional formations, focused on volitional formations, based upon volitional formations, being moistened by delight and lust—then consciousness grows, develops, and matures.
>
> Monks, someone may say: "Apart from form, apart from feeling, apart from perception, apart from volitional formations, I declare the coming and going of consciousness, its passing away and rebirth, its growth, development, and maturation."—but [in reality] that is something that will not happen.
>
> SN 22.54 – Seeds (Bīja Sutta)

Whenever the Buddha uses the term consciousness in his discourses, he never refers to an isolated consciousness. He always refers to a consciousness that is connected with form, feeling, perception, and volitional formations. How can a plant exist in a place without soil and water?

We learned all these details for the purpose of understanding the term bhava. Bhava has an extremely deep meaning that is impossible to understand if one uses merely a simplistic word such as "being," or "becoming," when translating the Dhamma from Pāli. But when we define bhava as the arranging of kamma to bear fruit, it helps us to understand that bhava is the cause of birth. When there is bhava, birth comes to be. With the cessation of bhava, birth ceases. With the arising of a cause, an effect comes to be. With the cessation of the cause, the effect ceases.

What Gives Rise to Bhava?

It is impossible for a person with ordinary knowledge to understand how the cycle of rebirth is formed internally within a life. The Buddha succeeded in understanding this because he followed a path consisting of virtue, concentration, and wisdom. Since the Buddha, no one else in the world thus far has come up with a solution to the problem of life in saṃsāra. The Dhamma shows the way to gradually solve this conundrum.

There is nothing in life that can be understood by praying with blind faith. The nature of life can only be realized by sustained, intelligent investigation.

Bhava Does Not Come to Be Without a Cause

The arranging of kamma to bear fruit (*bhava*) does not come to be without a cause; it is the result of a cause. The arranging of kamma to bear fruit (*bhava*) is subject to the law of causation, which means, when the cause ceases, the corresponding effect also ceases. Having investigated wisely to determine the cause that gives rise to bhava, the Buddha was able to find the exact cause.

Bhava Arises with Clinging as the Condition

> When there is clinging, bhava comes to be; bhava has clinging as its condition (*upādāna paccayā bhavo*).
>
> SN 12.10 – Gotama the Great Sakyan Sage (Gotama Sutta)

Chapter 8

Clinging

We must clearly understand the term clinging. When attempting to understand the law of Dependent Origination, we should understand the meaning of clinging devoid of an element of ownership, or a concept of someone who clings to something. But this does not mean that there are no beings or individuals. The Buddha never proclaimed that there are no beings and no individuals. Rather, he taught there is no self within a being or individual. In other words, a person does not have any control over conditioned things so as to wish "let this be thus" or "let this not be thus."

Once, venerable Moḷiyaphagguna asked the Buddha: "Venerable sir, is there a person who clings?" The notion of self is implicit in this question. As well, the idea that a self carries out clinging is implicit in this question. Therefore, the Buddha corrected the question before answering.

> "That is not a valid question," the Blessed One replied. "I do not say, 'One clings [to craving].' If I should say, 'One clings [to craving],' in that case this would be a valid question: 'Venerable sir, is there a person who clings?' But I do not speak thus. Since I do not speak thus, if one should ask me, 'Venerable sir, with what

> as condition does clinging come to be?' this would be a valid question. To this the valid answer is: 'With craving as condition, clinging comes to be…'"
>
> SN 12.12 – Moḷiyaphagguna (Moḷiyaphagguna Sutta)

Based on this explanation, if we are to realize the principle of cause and effect, then we must think in accordance with the principle of cause and effect. Clinging is a word which has a very clear meaning. It means getting attached or getting caught up, either very strongly or just slightly.

Clinging is the cause of bhava. Therefore, clinging is a powerful causal factor. Once, the Buddha explained the gravity of clinging to a person named Vacchagotta:

> I declare, Vaccha, rebirth for one with clinging, not for one without clinging. Vaccha, it is something like this: a fire burns with clinging [as fuel], not without clinging; Vaccha, in the same way, I declare rebirth for one with clinging [as fuel], not for one without clinging [as fuel].
>
> SN 44.9 – The Debating Hall (Kutuhalasālā Sutta)

Clinging

The arranging of kamma to bear fruit (*bhava*) arises due to clinging. The Buddha, with his great wisdom, discovered that clinging occurs in four ways:

(1). Clinging to sensual pleasures (*kāmūpādāna*)

(2). Clinging to views (*diṭṭhūpādāna*)

(3). Clinging to behaviors and observances (*sīlabbatūpādāna*)

(4). Clinging to the notion of "me," "mine," and "my self" (*attavādūpādāna*)

Saṃsāra, the endless round of birth and death, is formed within a life caught up in these four types of clinging. Beings are reborn in hell, the ghost world, the animal world, the human world, and heavenly realms because of the arranging of kamma to bear fruit (i.e., bhava) conditioned by these four types of clinging.

1. Clinging to Sensual Pleasures

All types of beings born in the sense sphere cling to objects of sensual pleasure. They are infatuated with and intoxicated by the five objects of sensual pleasure: namely forms, sounds, odors, flavors, and tangibles. Beings who are caught up in sensual pleasures commit all kinds of unwholesome acts, such as killing living beings, stealing, engaging in various forms of sexual misconduct, and consuming intoxicating drinks and drugs; they lie, speak divisively, use abusive language, and engage in idle chatter, are covetous and harbor ill will. All these unwholesome deeds are the result of clinging to sensual pleasures. Only the Buddha correctly defined sensual pleasures.

What is Sensual Pleasure?

> There are, monks, these five facets of sensual pleasure: forms cognizable by the eye that are desirable, pleasant, agreeable, pleasing, alluring, and arouse defilements; sounds cognizable by the ear ... odors cognizable by the nose ... flavors cognizable by the tongue ... tangibles cognizable by the body that are desirable, pleasant, agreeable, pleasing, alluring, and arouse defilements. However, monks, these are not sensual pleasures; in the noble Dhamma, these are called "facets of sensual pleasure."

> A person's sensual pleasure is lustful thoughts; the beautiful things in the world are not sensual pleasures. A person's sensual pleasure is the lust that arises in one's thoughts. The beautiful things remain just as they are in the world, but the brave and wise eliminate the desire for them.
>
> AN 6.63 – Penetrative (Nibbedhika Sutta)

Now the nature of sensual pleasure is clear to us. Sensual pleasure is becoming infatuated with captivating objects of sensual pleasure. This clearly emphasizes the Buddha's thorough investigation of sensual pleasures. Therefore, clinging to sensual pleasures is actually getting caught up in harboring lustful intentions toward the objects of sensual pleasure—forms, sounds, odors, flavors, and tangibles.

The Iron Chain

In the time of the Buddha, some monks who were walking for alms in the city of Sāvatthi saw a group of prisoners bound by iron chains. They informed the Buddha of this disturbing sight, and the Buddha's reply was a real eye-opener for the monks:

> There do exist bonds made of iron, wood, and rushes, but the wise do not consider them to be strong bonds. Having a strong attachment and passion for gems, jewelry, earrings, wives and children, and longing for them—that is what the wise consider to be the strong bond. That bond, subtle and hard to escape, drags one to the plane of misery.
>
> SN 3.10 – Bondage (Bandhana Sutta)

Seeing Suffering as Pleasure

Ordinary beings experience endless suffering in their pursuit of sensual pleasures. Yet they only think of the gratification of sensual pleasures and see pleasure in them always. As a result, they experience infinite suffering. Still, they disregard the suffering and pursue gratification of the senses.

See the Reality of Sensual Pleasures

The Buddha taught us that we should understand the gratification (*assāda*) of sensual pleasures as gratification, the danger (*ādinava*) of sensual pleasures as danger, and the escape (*nissaraṇa*) from sensual pleasures as escape. Some people with limited intelligence have misinterpreted this teaching. They claim that one must indulge in sensual pleasures as much as possible to understand the gratification of sensual pleasures. They neither talk about the danger of sensual pleasures nor the escape from them. Those holding such a wrong view are capable of distorting the truth in any manner to suit their purpose. But one who investigates with wisdom in an impartial manner is able to clearly see how beings suffer because of sensual pleasures.

The True Nature of Sensual Pleasures

The Blessed One taught that sensual pleasures provide very little gratification, much greater suffering and despair, and that the danger in them is still more. He instructed his disciples who wished to escape from the bondage of saṃsāra to investigate the dangers of sensual pleasures and be free of them:

> The Blessed One has stated that sensual pleasures provide very little gratification, much suffering and

despair, and that the danger in them is still more. With the simile of the skeleton ... with the simile of the piece of meat ... with the simile of the grass torch ... with the simile of the pit of coals ... with the simile of the dream ... with the simile of the borrowed goods ... with the simile of fruits on a tree ... with the simile of the butcher's knife and block... with the simile of the stake ... with the simile of the snake's head, the Blessed One has stated that sensual pleasures provide very little gratification, much suffering and despair, and that the danger in them is still more.

MN 22 – The Simile of the Snake (Alagaddūpama Sutta)

Blinded by Sensual Pleasures

King Ajātasattu, blinded by the lust for power and sensual pleasure, committed the heinous act (*ānantariya kamma*) of killing his father. Devadatta, blinded by the pursuit of sensual pleasures, committed a similarly heinous act by injuring the Buddha. Queen Māgandiyā harbored hatred toward the Buddha and accumulated a great deal of demerit because she was blinded by the gratification in sensual pleasures. The youth Nanda raped the Arahant Nun Uppalavaṇṇā and ended up in hell due to his infatuation with sensual pleasures. Cunda the pig farmer, caught up in sensual pleasures, spent his whole life slaughtering pigs for a living until he died miserably. Thus, one who is blinded by the desire for sensual pleasure is unable to distinguish between what is wholesome and unwholesome. He is unable to distinguish between good and bad. Shame and fear of wrongdoing and respect for moral values are disregarded in the blind pursuit of sensual pleasures.

Do Not Be Blinded by Sensual Pleasures

The Buddha used disparaging terms to describe sensual pleasures:

> Monks, "fear" is a term for sensual pleasures. "Suffering" is a term for sensual pleasures. "Disease" is a term for sensual pleasures. "Boil" is a term for sensual pleasures. "Attachment" is a term for sensual pleasures. "Mud" is a term for sensual pleasures.
>
> AN 6.23 – Peril (Bhaya Sutta)

> And what, monks, is the result of sensual pleasures? Monks, if something is desired, then, either as a result of merit or demerit, there is the arising of various [forms of] existence. This, monks, is called the result of sensual pleasures.
>
> AN 6.63 – Penetrative (Nibbedhika Sutta)

The destiny of beings caught up in the gratification of sensual pleasures is the creation of bhava, which causes rebirth and prolongs the wandering in saṃsāra.

2. Clinging to Views

We often hear and read about various ideas, attitudes, and views. And in most instances, we tend to accept and cling to these views without due consideration. Once, a wanderer named Dīghanakha (Aggivessana by clan name) came to the Buddha and expressed an interesting idea:

> Master Gotama, I am a person who holds such a view as this—that is, the view: "I dislike everything."

The Buddha's reply was an eye-opener for him:

> Aggivessana, this view of yours: "I dislike everything," do you dislike that view as well?
>
> MN 74 – To Dīghanakha (Dīghanakha Sutta)

It is because of clinging to views that people get caught up in conclusions arrived at by thinking along various reckless, ill-contrived points of debate. Wrong views always arise because of clinging to views.

Getting Caught up in the Extremes "All Exists" and "All Does Not Exist"

> Kaccāna, these beings of the world for the most part dwell with two views: existence (permanent existence after death) and non-existence (beings cease to exist and are annihilated after death).... Kaccāna, the view: "All exists" is one extreme. The view: "All does not exist" is the other extreme.
>
> SN 12.15 – Kaccānagotta (Kaccānagotta Sutta)

The extreme view "all exists" gives rise to the view of eternalism (*sassata diṭṭhi*)—the view that there exists within oneself a soul that will become eternal after death. This soul that is created as an act of god would after death be sent either to heaven or hell forever, as per the wish of god. That soul is permanent, eternal, and everlasting. When a person gets caught up in this utterly false view, he or she is capable of committing any violent act.

Caught in the Extreme "All Does Not Exist"

The other extreme is the view "all does not exist." This extreme view is related to materialism. It is similar to the idea that when the parts of a machine are assembled it is able to produce energy; when the parts are disassembled, the energy ceases to exist. Similarly, those who hold the view that "all does not exist" believe a being is merely the product of a biochemical process and nothing else. Those who hold this extreme view do not believe in kamma and its results. They do not accept the fact that life is based on consciousness and other related mental factors.

They say: "Life exists only until death. It is absurd to think of a life after death. Therefore, if there are any comforts and happiness to be enjoyed in this life, they have to be experienced here and now, even by taking out loans. With death, the breakup of the body, beings are destroyed and cease to exist." This is the view of annihilationism (*uccheda diṭṭhi*). Even in the time of the Buddha, this was a popular view in India.

In the time of the Buddha, there was an ascetic by the name of Ajita Kesakambali who established a religious sect for the sole purpose of promoting this view. He was an annihilationist who wore a blanket of human hair. He taught that one should never think of life after death. If a person were to give gifts piled up from one end of the Ganges River to the other, still it would not yield any merit. In the same way, if a person were to slaughter people and heap up the dead bodies from one end of the Ganges River to the other, that would not yield any demerit. There is no point in attending to parents; children are merely the byproduct of their enjoyment. Hence, they do not have to be respected on that account. Ajita Kesakambali further said that wholesome actions such as developing the mind, practicing virtue, and developing meditation are absurd activities. He ridiculed the idea of spontaneous birth in heaven and hell, claiming it was impossible for anyone to prove such a thing. Even today, irrespective of religion, there are many who are caught up in this view. In particular, they do not accept religious doctrines. Even if they do show some fondness toward their religion, it is only to gain some social standing or personal benefit, not with the honest idea of gaining any understanding of life.

The World Is Dominated by the Extreme View "All Does Not Exist"

Most of the political philosophies of the present-day are influenced by the view of "all does not exist" (i.e., annihilation after death). Marxism, Capitalism, so-called Democracy—all of these political philosophies are connected to the view of annihilationism. Those political parties that do not believe in merit and demerit have subjected humanity to great oppression and exploitation. They strive to achieve their political objectives by exploiting human differences based on race, ethnicity, and color. They are prepared to commit any unlawful act, slaughter human beings, and initiate armed conflicts due to their clinging to the view of annihilation after death.

Wrong Views

Clinging to views leads to blind faith in all types of superstitious practices such as reading horoscopes, palmistry, astrology, belief in auspicious times, and good omens, etc. It is not possible to grasp the truth when one clings to such wrong views. Those who cling strongly to wrong views are far away from seeing the truth. They lack the strength and willpower to break free from these wrong views. Unfortunately, they seek solace in mysterious solutions rather than building a good life in a practical way. Hence, one should understand the danger of clinging to views (*diṭṭhupādāna*). Furthermore, kamma is arranged to bear fruit as a result of clinging to these views.

Escaping Both the Extremes of "All Exists" and "All Does Not Exist"

Almost the entire human race clings to either the extreme "all exists" or "all does not exist." All the suffering and despair in the world is a result of clinging to these extreme views. Therefore, the Buddha instructed us to avoid the extreme "all exists," which is eternalism, and the extreme "all does not exist," which is annihilationism, and instead realize how causes result in effects. Therefore, the Buddha's teachings stress the need to achieve right view. The Buddha saw with his characteristic wisdom that if right view is not achieved, beings who get caught up in clinging to views lead themselves toward suffering by the arranging of kamma under the influence of ignorance.

3. Clinging to Behaviors and Observances

The nature of this type of clinging is for one to get attached to various behaviors and observances with the belief that they will lead to well-being. The virtue introduced by the Buddha leads to righteous bodily and verbal actions that result in harmonious and peaceful lives. There is nothing weird or unnatural in the virtue shown by the Buddha. The outcome of a virtuous life is sense restraint, peace, and calm.

Virtue for a disciple of the Buddha means abstaining from using weapons, harming living beings, taking intoxicants, intentional killing of living beings, theft, bribery, and corruption. The Blessed One instructed his disciples to develop a virtuous life and avoid sexual misconduct that goes against the moral standards of society. He instructed disciples to avoid all kinds of verbal unwholesomeness such as lying, deceit, divisive speech, and abusive language. The Buddha advised lay disciples to keep these precepts on a daily basis.

Virtue Is a Beautiful Thing

In addition, on full-moon days, lay disciples are encouraged to observe eight precepts, emulating the lives of Arahants, wherein disciples abstain from the use of luxurious seats and beds, consuming food after noon, decorating the body and applying perfumes, and entertainment such as dancing, singing, listening to music, and watching films and dramas. In this way, a disciple observes the precepts not searching for any enigmatic benefit, but with the sole purpose of developing an essential aspect of the Noble Eightfold Path.

When One Fails to Understand Virtue

A person who fails to understand virtue as taught by the Buddha will get caught in various behaviors and observances in the name of virtue. The color of the clothes one wears does not represent virtue in any way. But some consider dressing up in white garments and simple clothing as part of virtue. Also, some consider abstaining from dying their hair and painting their nails as part of virtue. In this way, they refrain from beautifying themselves and blame and disparage others who do, in an attempt to exalt what they consider to be virtuous. Apart from days when eight precepts are observed, the Buddha did not lay down any precepts for lay disciples to abstain from adorning one's body, wearing ornaments, using perfumes, and beautifying with cosmetics.

Some people mistakenly believe that vegetarianism constitutes a precept. When they cling strongly to this view, they insult and scorn people who are not vegetarian. They project themselves as ideal examples of mercy and kindness. In the time of the Buddha, the disciples of Nigaṇṭha Nātaputta (the Jains) used to do this. But insulting and criticizing others must not be the outcome of the practice of noble virtue.

During the time of the Buddha, some people who practiced austerities were strongly attached to extreme behaviors and observances. Some of them did not eat food cooked or offered by women. Others did not accept food from houses where funeral rites were being conducted, or from houses where girls had reached puberty, saying the food was impure. Some ate food that was blessed with religious rituals while others ate food that had been offered to devas.

At present, some people practice an observance where on Fridays they only eat fruit and drink milk. Others at auspicious times lay the foundation for houses and conduct opening ceremonies. Despite adhering to auspicious times, there is no shortage of political unrest, conflict, immoral behavior, and violence. Boiling milk at an auspicious time is another common ritual. Some people follow an observance wherein they bathe in the water to wash away their bad kamma. Some people bathe at auspicious times after placing herbal leaves on their head and under their feet.

Some people commence work and carry out financial transactions at auspicious times as an observance. Some people perform firewalking at an auspicious time. Some pierce their body with spikes. Some people do not cremate dead bodies on Tuesdays and Fridays. Wrong view (*micchā diṭṭhi*) is the basis for this wrong grasp of behaviors and observances. Even the tenfold mundane right view is absent in the lives of people who follow these behaviors and observances.

There are instances where people behave like dogs when they are deluded and cling to extreme behaviors and observances based on wrong view. This is called the practice of behaving like a dog (*kukkuravata*). There are also people who observe the practice of behaving like a goat (*ajavata*) and others who follow the practice of behaving like a cow (*govata*). Clinging to these behaviors and observances results in the accumulation of kamma based on ignorance. In this way, clinging to behaviors and observances gives rise to the arranging of kamma to bear fruit (*upādāna paccayā bhavo*).

4. Clinging to the Notion of Self

Clinging to the notion of self is an extremely strong bond. It means clinging to the deeply rooted notion in the mind of "me, mine, and my self." This clinging leads to the idea that there exists in one's life an eternal soul that can be considered "my self," which can be controlled according to one's own will and considered as belonging to oneself.

Just like a huge banyan tree with its branches and roots spread out in all directions, this concept of a soul spreads throughout our life. Arahants were the only ones to extirpate this view, which is an utter fabrication of the mind, yet appears to be a truth from all angles. All other beings remain deluded and bound by this notion of self to a greater or lesser degree.

When clinging exists in the four ways explained above, the arranging of kamma to bear fruit (i.e., bhava) results. The nature of the law of cause and effect is such that when causes arise, so do the corresponding effects; and when causes cease, the effects also cease. Thus, when there is clinging, bhava comes to be.

The Arahant

The above four types of clinging are nonexistent within the Arahant, a fully enlightened one, who has achieved supreme wisdom in the Buddha's path. Arahants are found only in the Buddha's Dispensation. In an Arahant, clinging has been completely eradicated. Because clinging has ceased, the arranging of kamma to bear fruit (bhava) has also ceased. Because bhava has ceased, birth has also ceased. Thus, when one is free from birth, one is forever free from aging-and-death and the whole mass of suffering.

The Non-Returner

Disciples of the Buddha who have attained the fruition of non-returning, (*anāgāmi*), are completely devoid of three types of clinging—clinging to sensual pleasures, clinging to views, and clinging to behaviors and observances. With respect to clinging to the notion of self, the twenty-fold self-view is also absent in the non-returner. However, the notion of "me, mine, and my self" still exists internally within the non-returner as a latent disposition.

It is something like this: when a dirty cloth has been washed with soap, the cloth is clean, but the smell of soap remains. But when this cloth is folded and kept in a cupboard with fragrance, the smell of soap goes away as well.

The underlying tendency to the notion of "me, mine, and my self" within the non-returner is like the smell of soap in the washed cloth. Since the non-returner is devoid of clinging to sensual pleasures, there is no arranging of kamma to bear fruit in the sense sphere. Accordingly, for a non-returner there is no birth in the sense sphere. Yet, because of the latent disposition to the notion of "me and mine," the non-returner's consciousness, volition, and aspiration will become established in either the form sphere or the formless sphere. Therefore, there will be the creation of either the form sphere or formless sphere, and accordingly birth into the form or formless Brahma worlds will occur. There the non-returner will fully uproot the notion of "me, mine, and my self," thereby destroying the only remaining type of clinging and resulting in the cessation of bhava—the attainment of Nibbāna.

The Once-Returner

Clinging to sensual pleasures is not that strong in disciples of the Buddha who have attained the second stage of Enlightenment, which is once-returning (*sakadāgāmī*). However, clinging to sensual pleasures has not been completely eradicated. Once-returners are completely free of clinging to views and clinging to behaviors and observances. The twenty-fold self-view has also been eliminated; though the notion of "me, mine, and my self" still remains within the once-returner, he is aware that it is a delusion. He knows this deceptive notion that arises within the mind exists due to ignorance. Therefore, he strives to get rid of ignorance and gain realization. Since the once-returner still clings to sensual pleasures to some extent, there is still the arranging of kamma to bear fruit in the sense sphere. Because of the creation of the sense sphere, a once-returner will be reborn in the sense sphere. A once-returner therefore will be born one more time in either the human world or the heavenly world and there make an end of suffering.

The Stream-Enterer

The stream-enterer (*sotāpanna* disciple) is the person who has achieved the first fruition of the Noble Eightfold Path through spiritual development.

In the Pāli language, *sota* means "stream" and refers to the Noble Eightfold Path; *āpanna* means the "person who has entered." This disciple is called the stream-enterer with the idea that the disciple has entered the Noble Eightfold Path.

Although the stream-enterer still clings to sensual pleasures, he is able to recognize not only the gratification but also the danger of sensual pleasures. He has a considerable understanding about the escape from sensual pleasures, which is the relief gained by eradicating desire and lust toward sensual pleasures. Moreover, stream-enterers are free of clinging to views, clinging to behaviors and observances, and the twenty-fold self-view has also been eliminated. Clinging to the notion of "me, mine, and my self" still remains within the stream-enterer, yet he is aware that that notion is untrue and wrong. He knows that "whatever is subject to origination is all subject to cessation (*yaṃ kiñci samudaya dhammaṃ, sabbaṃ taṃ nirodha dhammaṃ*)." Since the stream-enterer still clings to sensual pleasures, he continues to live a peaceful and righteous life amid sensual pleasures while caring for his family. He has eradicated clinging to views, clinging to behaviors and observances, and the twenty-fold self-view. As a result, kamma that could take him to a bad destination such as the animal world, ghost world, *asura* world, or hell is not generated within him.

Therefore, all the disciples who have attained the fruitions of the path are freed from the danger of being born in the planes of misery. Through the Buddha's marvelous wisdom, he realized that the cycle of rebirth is created by the arranging of kamma to bear fruit, which in turn is caused by clinging (*upādāna paccayā bhavo*).

Objects of Clinging

The Buddha explained clinging in this way:

> Monks, I will teach you about the things that cause clinging and about clinging itself. Listen to that attentively.
>
> Monks, what are the things that cause clinging? What is clinging? The eye, monks, is a thing that causes clinging; the desire and lust for it is the clinging there. The ear ... The nose ... The tongue is a thing that causes clinging; the desire and lust for it is the clinging there ... The body ... The mind is a thing that causes clinging; the desire and lust for it is the clinging there. These, monks, are called the things that cause clinging, and this is clinging.

SN 35.110 Things That Can Be Clung To (Upādāna Sutta)

The Path to Nibbāna in Brief

Once, a monk approached the Buddha and asked him to teach the Dhamma in brief to help him be free from suffering. The Buddha said:

> Monk, in creating an attachment one is bound to Māra; in not creating an attachment, one is freed from the Evil One.

The monk was clever in instantly understanding the Dhamma taught briefly by the Buddha.

> "Understood, Blessed One! Understood, Fortunate One!"
>
> "In what way, monk, did you understand in detail the meaning of the Dhamma that was stated by me in brief?"
>
> "In creating an attachment to form (which is conditioned by the four great elements), venerable sir, one is bound to Māra; by not creating an attachment to form one is freed from the Evil One. In creating an attachment to feeling one is bound to Māra; by not creating an attachment to feeling (which is conditioned by contact) one is freed from the Evil One ... to perception (which is conditioned by contact) ... In creating an attachment to volitional formations (which are conditioned by contact) one is bound to Māra; by not creating an attachment to volitional formations, one is freed from the Evil One ... In creating an attachment to consciousness (which is conditioned by name-and-form) one is bound to Māra;

by not creating an attachment to consciousness one is freed from the Evil One."

SN 22.63 – In Clinging (Upādiya Sutta)

The Buddha praised the monk for being intelligent enough to quickly understand in detail the Dhamma that he had explained in brief. The Buddha further advised the monk to make use of the same Dhamma to attain full realization.

True Guidance

This amazing discovery of the Buddha was not restricted to his personal well-being, nor was it only a truth of personal relevance. As well, it was not a mysterious formula he derived philosophically. It was not a deception to scare people into becoming his followers. It was not a system of logical arguments designed to counter those who held different views. The Buddha dedicated his life to helping his disciples realize the Dhamma in exactly the same way that he had realized it.

Like a skilled farmer who would first select the fertile ground suitable for cultivation, the Buddha paid special attention to those who became his disciples. He disciplined them in the path of Dhamma with a great deal of attention. His disciples too, guided their lives accordingly along the path of Dhamma. In the end, just like the Buddha, they too succeeded in escaping from all clinging. This is a genuine reality experienced by millions of disciples among devas and humans.

The Buddha, who completely freed himself from clinging, eradicated the cause of clinging with full understanding. The Buddha revealed that clinging does not arise due to the will of a god or due to one's own wish—both of these ideas are wrong views. He proclaimed that clinging arises due to a cause.

What Is the Cause of Clinging?

The Buddha, the one with amazing wisdom, successfully solved this problem successfully, and he also revealed the solution to devas and humans. How clinging comes to be is no longer a mystery. We are gradually beginning to understand the components of our lives oppressed by the suffering brought about by the principle of cause and effect.

> When there is craving, clinging comes to be; clinging has craving as its condition (*taṇhā paccayā upādānaṃ*).
>
> SN 12.10 – Gotama the Great Sakyan Sage (Gotama Sutta)

[illegible]

[illegible]

What is the Cause of Change?

The Buddha, the one who [illegible] solved this problem [illegible] solution [illegible] Change [illegible]

[illegible]

[illegible]

Chapter 9

Craving

In the very first discourse of the Buddha after attaining Enlightenment, the Buddha revealed craving as the fundamental cause of life's problems, i.e., the cause of suffering.

> Now this, monks, is the noble truth of the origin of suffering: it is this craving which leads to renewed existence (*ponobhavikā*), having the nature of adhering with desire (*nandirāgasahagatā*), delighting in each and every birth (*tatra tatrābhinandini*), namely:
>
> (1). Craving for sensual pleasures (*kāmataṇhā*—craving for forms, sounds, odors, flavors, and tangibles)
>
> (2). Craving for existence (*bhavataṇhā*—believing one's life to be "me, mine, and my self" and craving for a continued existence of a self)
>
> (3). Craving for non-existence (*vibhavataṇhā*—the deep-rooted craving for this mind, body, and everything else not to exist. When this craving becomes prominent, it causes rebirth in the formless realms and the impercipient realm)
>
> SN 56.11 – Setting in Motion the Wheel of the Dhamma (Dhammacakkappavattana Sutta)

The Buddha, who eradicated craving, emphatically stated that these three types of craving must be eradicated in order to achieve complete peace in life.

Investigate and Understand

At first glance, a person who lives an ordinary life will not see that these three forms of craving exist within him. Rarely does one realize that one is caught up in the fast-acting nature of craving.

This is because many people do not get an opportunity in their lives to listen to the true Dhamma that requires deep study and investigation. One who is naturally inclined toward gratification lives with the constant fear of losing that gratification of the senses. A life afflicted by ignorance and shrouded by self-view is not easily directed toward realization.

Yet, if someone directs his wisdom in line with a true teaching, he alone will succeed in developing the Noble Eightfold Path to fully realize the Four Noble Truths, and thereby gain ultimate peace in life.

Seeing the Truth Results in Disenchantment

Generally, for most people, just the thought of getting rid of craving scares them. But if someone saw the nature of craving, the suffering caused due to craving, how craving conditions clinging, how clinging conditions the arranging of kamma to bear fruit, and how the arranging of kamma to bear fruit causes birth, propelling beings headlong into the misery of saṃsāra—the endless cycle of birth and death—such a person would never relish the continued existence of craving.

One day, a certain deva came to the Buddha and asked: "Who created beings?"

The Blessed One provided a precise answer, saying: "Craving created beings."

The Buddha did not give these answers based on knowledge heard and learned from someone else. He did not possess knowledge learned from anyone else. There arose within the Buddha the vision and knowledge of Dhamma, unheard of before in his life, which is why the Buddha's knowledge is declared pubbe ananussutesu dhammesu. This is exactly why the Buddha possessed a marvelous realization.

What Is Craving?

> Monks, what is craving? Monks, craving arises in six ways: there arises craving for forms, there arises craving for sounds, there arises craving for odors, there arises craving for flavors, there arises craving for tangibles, there arises craving for mental phenomena. This, monks, is called craving.
>
> SN 12.2 – Analysis of Dependent Origination (Vibhaṅga Sutta)

Once the Buddha was asked:

> What is the arrow that has pierced deep into this life?

The Buddha's reply was very clear:

> Craving is the arrow that has pierced deep into this life.
>
> SN 1.66 – Afflicted (Attahata Sutta)

Where Beings Dwell

Monks, devas and humans dwell in forms, they are attached to forms, they delight in forms. With the change of forms, having to let go and eliminate the desire for forms, devas and humans dwell in suffering.

SN 35.136 – Delight in Forms (Gayha Sutta)

Thus, One Suffers

Monks, devas and humans dwell in sounds, they are attached to sounds, they delight in sounds. With the change of sounds, having to let go and eliminate the desire for sounds, devas and humans dwell in suffering. Monks, devas and humans dwell in odors, they are attached to odors, they delight in odors. With the change of odors, having to let go and eliminate the desire for odors, devas and humans dwell in suffering. Monks, devas and humans dwell in flavors, they are attached to flavors, they delight in flavors. With the change of flavors, having to let go and eliminate the desire for flavors, devas and humans dwell in suffering. Monks, devas and humans dwell in tangibles, they are attached to tangibles, they delight in tangibles. With the change of tangibles, having to let go and eliminate the desire for tangibles, devas and humans dwell in suffering. Monks, devas and humans dwell in mental phenomena, they are attached to mental phenomena, they delight in mental phenomena. With the change of mental phenomena, having to let go and eliminate the desire for mental phenomena, devas and humans dwell in suffering.

SN 35.136 – Delight in Forms (Gayha Sutta)

Only the individual who has the ability to understand life deeply will succeed in understanding that beings suffer due to craving. Desire can lead one's whole life toward utter ruin and immense suffering.

The Fatal Disease of Life

> Monks, craving is a disease, craving is a pus-oozing boil, craving is a spike.... Monks, if something is considered as "I," with the notion of self; if one considers "I exist" in something, with the notion of self; if one considers "I exist" apart from something, with the notion of self; if one considers something as "mine," with the notion of self—what happens is contrary to such notions. Beings of the world attached to existence that is subject to change seek delight in that very same existence.
>
> SN 35.91 – Being Stirred (2) (Dutiya Ejā Sutta)

Worldly life is based on desire. Therefore, farsighted thinking is not present in ordinary life. The Buddha understood how beings of the world imprisoned within narrow thinking patterns face various hardships, conflicts, quarrels, and even loss of life—all of which arise because of craving.

The Links Created by Desire

> Thus, Ānanda, because of feeling craving arises; because of craving there is seeking; because of seeking there is gain; because of gain there is arriving at a decision about what was gained; because of arriving at a decision there is attaching with desire; because of attaching with desire there is the mind's immersion in what was gained, with the thought: "It is mine;" because

> of the mind's immersion in what was gained, with the thought: "It is mine," there is the arising of the sense of ownership in the mind; because of the arising of the sense of ownership in the mind there arises stinginess; because of stinginess there is safeguarding what was gained; because of the struggle to safeguard what was gained, various evil unwholesome phenomena originate—the taking up of clubs and weapons, conflicts, antagonism and quarrels, puerile scolding, divisive speech, and lying.
>
> DN 15 – The Great Discourse on Causation
> (Mahānidāna Sutta)

It is when we study these discourses of the Buddha that we can understand at least to some extent the seriousness of craving. Craving exists like a cancer that has metastasized in all directions. Because of his amazing realization, the Buddha was able to discover how sorrow and suffering originate due to craving.

Craving and Desire in the Journey of Saṃsāra

> Monks, I will teach you about craving—the net, widespread, pervasive, and stuck in all places, by which the beings of this world have been tangled, wrapped, and by which they have become like a tangled skein, a mass of thread dipped in porridge, a mass of reeds and rushes in disarray; they dwell unable to go beyond this perilous saṃsāra, with its plane of misery, the bad destinations, the place of sorrow. Listen and contemplate properly; I will speak.

"Yes, venerable sir," those monks replied. The Blessed One said this:

"And how, monks, because of craving—the net, widespread, pervasive, and stuck in all places, by which the beings of this world have been tangled, wrapped, and by which they have become like a tangled skein, a mass of thread dipped in porridge, a mass of reeds and rushes in disarray—are beings unable to go beyond this perilous saṃsāra, with its plane of misery, the bad destinations, the place of sorrow?"

AN 4.199 – Craving (Taṇhā Jālinī Sutta)

The Nature of Craving that Consumes Life

There are, monks, eighteen workings of craving grasping to oneself and eighteen workings of craving grasping to the external.

Monks, what are the eighteen workings of craving grasping to oneself? When there is the notion (1) "I am," there arises the notion (2) "I am thus." There arises the notion (3) "I am just so." There arises the notion (4) "I am otherwise." There arises the notion (5) "I am destructible." There arises the notion (6) "I am indestructible." There arises the notion (7) "Does there exist such a person as me?" There arises the notion (8) "Do I exist in this way?" There arises the notion (9) "Do I exist thus?" There arises the notion (10) "Do I exist otherwise?" There arises the notion (11) "Does there exist a person as me?" There arises the notion (12) "Can I exist in this way?" There arises the notion (13) "Can

I exist thus?" There arises the notion (14) "Can I exist otherwise?" There arises the notion (15) "In the future shall I be?" There arises the notion (16) "In the future shall I be in this way?" There arises the notion (17) "Shall I be thus?" There arises the notion (18) "Shall I be otherwise?"

AN 4.199 – Craving (Taṇhā Jālinī Sutta)

Craving Grasping to the External

Monks, what are the eighteen workings of craving grasping to the external? When there is the notion: (1) "I am of these forms," there arises the notion: (2) "I am thus because of these forms." There arises the notion: (3) "I am just so because of these forms." There arises the notion: (4) "I am otherwise because of these forms." There arises the notion: (5) "I am indestructible because of these forms." There arises the notion: (6) "I am destructible." There arises the notion: (7) "Because of these forms, is there such a person as me?" There arises the notion: (8) "Because of these forms, am I in this way?" There arises the notion: (9) "Because of these forms, am I thus?" There arises the notion: (10) "Because of these forms, am I otherwise?" There arises the notion: (11) "Because of these forms, can there be a person as I?" There arises the notion: (12) "Because of these forms, can I be in this way?" There arises the notion: (13) "Because of these forms, can I be thus?" There arises the notion: (14) "Because of these forms, can I be otherwise?" There arises the notion: (15) "Because of these forms, shall I be in the future?" There arises the notion: (16) "Because of these forms, shall I be in this way?" There arises the notion: (17) "Because of these forms, shall I be thus?" There arises the notion: (18) "Because of these forms, shall I be otherwise?" Monks, these are the eighteen workings of craving grasping to the external.

AN 4.199 – Craving (Taṇhā Jālinī Sutta)

Craving Works in 108 Ways

Thus, there are eighteen workings of craving grasping to oneself, and eighteen workings of craving grasping to the external. These are called the thirty-six workings of craving. Thus, there are thirty-six such workings of craving pertaining to the past, thirty-six workings of craving arising in the future, and thirty-six workings of craving pertaining to the present. Thus, there are one hundred and eight workings of craving.

This, monks, is that craving—the net, widespread, pervasive, and stuck in all places, by which the beings of this world have been tangled, wrapped, and by which they have become like a tangled skein, a mass of thread dipped in porridge, a mass of reeds and rushes in disarray; they dwell unable to go beyond this perilous saṃsāra, with its plane of misery, the bad destinations, the place of sorrow.

AN 4.199 – Craving (Taṇhā Jālinī Sutta)

Where Are These Desires Born?

Monks, if this craving arises, where does it arise? If craving establishes itself, where does it become established? If in this world there is anything that is agreeable and pleasurable, if this craving arises, it arises there; if this craving establishes itself, it becomes established there. And what in the world is agreeable and pleasurable?

The eye in the world is agreeable and pleasurable, if this craving arises, it arises there; if this craving establishes itself, it becomes established there. The ear in the world ... The nose in the world ... The tongue in the world ... The body in the world ... The mind in the world is agreeable and pleasurable, if this craving arises, it arises there; if this craving establishes itself, it becomes established there.

Forms in the world are agreeable and pleasurable, if this craving arises, it arises there; if this craving establishes itself, it becomes established there.... Sounds in the world ... Odors in the world ... Flavors in the world ... Tangibles in the world ... Mental phenomena in the world are agreeable and pleasurable, if this craving arises, it arises there; if this craving establishes itself, it becomes established there.

Eye-consciousness in the world is agreeable and pleasurable, if this craving arises, it arises there; if this craving establishes itself, it becomes established there.... Ear-consciousness in the world ... Nose-consciousness in the world ... Tongue-consciousness in the world ... Body-consciousness in the world ... Mind-consciousness in the world is agreeable and pleasurable, if this craving arises, it arises there; if this craving establishes itself, it becomes established there.

Eye-contact in the world is agreeable and pleasurable, if this craving arises, it arises there; if this craving establishes itself, it becomes established there.... Ear-contact in the world ... Nose-contact in the world ... Tongue-contact in the world ... Body-contact in the world ... Mind-contact in the world is agreeable and pleasurable, if this craving arises, it arises there; if this craving establishes itself, it becomes established there.

Feeling born of eye-contact in the world is agreeable and pleasurable, if this craving arises, it arises there; if this craving establishes itself, it becomes established there.... Feeling born of ear-contact in the world ... Feeling born of nose-contact in the world ... Feeling born of tongue-contact in the world ... Feeling born of body-contact in the world ... Feeling born of mind-contact in the world is agreeable and pleasurable, if this craving arises, it arises there; if this craving establishes itself, it becomes established there.

DN 22 – The Greater Discourse on the Establishments of Mindfulness (Mahāsatipaṭṭhāna Sutta)

Craving—The Seamstress

Contact, monks, is one end; the arising of contact is the second end; the cessation of contact is the middle; and craving is the seamstress. For craving sews together contact and the arising of contact to bring about rebirth in this or that state of existence. Monks, by this alone a monk specifically understands what should be specifically understood, fathoms and understands what should be fathomed and understood, and by specifically understanding what should be specifically understood, fathoming and understanding what should be fathomed and understood, in this very life he makes an end of suffering.

AN 6.61 – Middle (Majjhe Sutta)

The Buddha clearly stated that it is craving that creates the beings (*taṇhā janeti purisaṃ*) of the world; it is craving that raises the beings of the world to suffering, and it is craving that drags the beings of the world from one existence to another.

The True Problem Is Craving

In this way, craving is the main cause of both present and future conflict, unrest, corruption, deceit, crimes, violence, and terrorism in the world.

For the first time in the history of humankind, the Buddha discovered the source of all the problems in life, through what was truly the greatest scientific research, but which did not involve the use of any external physical equipment. There is no place within this discovery for a theory of creation by a god, a theory of a permanent self, or materialism.

There is no creator god in the world capable of challenging the amazing wisdom of the Buddha. He precisely and practically identified craving as the fundamental cause of suffering and having begun to wisely investigate the cause of craving, the Buddha finally succeeded in discovering the cause of craving as well.

What Gives Rise to Craving?

The Buddha did not approve of accepting anything with blind faith and being enslaved by it. What he valued was an investigative intellect.

> Then, monks, it occurred to me: "When what exists does craving come to be? By what is craving conditioned?" Then, monks, when I contemplated thoroughly with wisdom, I realized with wisdom: "When there is feeling, craving comes to be; craving has feeling as its condition (*vedanā paccayā taṇhā*)."
>
> SN 12.10 – Gotama the Great Sakyan Sage (Gotama Sutta)

The Reason for Craving

Craving is not something that arises without a cause. It is not an innate characteristic of the mind. Rather, craving is conditioned by feeling; one does not crave for something that one cannot feel. Hence, craving always arises toward something that one feels.

> And what, monks, is the source of that craving? From what does it originate? From what is it born? From what does it come to be? The source of that craving is feeling. It originates from feeling. It is born from feeling. It comes to be from feeling.
>
> SN 12.11 – Nutriment (Āhāra Sutta)

Chapter 10

Feeling

> And why, monks, do you call it feeling? Monks, with the meaning: "One feels," it is called feeling. And what does one feel? One feels pleasure, one feels pain, one feels neither-pain-nor-pleasure.
>
> SN 22.79 – Being Devoured (Khajjanīya Sutta)

Feeling Is an Iron Spike

Whatever feeling arises, whether it is pleasant, painful, or neither-painful-nor-pleasant, the ordinary being is deluded, tricked, and infatuated by the feeling. One who has not understood the nature of feeling is incapable of any other reaction besides being deluded and infatuated by feeling. Because of this woeful state of affairs in life, the Buddha likened feeling to an iron spike. He said:

> Monks, when the uninstructed worldling comes into contact with a painful feeling, he sorrows. He faints. He laments. He weeps beating his breast. He loses his mind. He feels two feelings—a bodily one and a mental one. Monks, it is something like this: a person is struck by a spike, then he is struck close to the same spot by a

second spike. Then, monks, that person feels a feeling caused by two spikes.

Similarly, monks, when the uninstructed worldling comes into contact with a painful feeling, he sorrows. He faints. He laments. He weeps beating his breast. He loses his mind. He feels two feelings—a bodily one and a mental one.

SN 36.6 – The Dart (Salla Sutta)

If One Does Not Know the Truth

When he comes into contact with painful feeling, he becomes angry. In he who harbors anger born of painful feeling, if there is a certain latent disposition toward aversion born of painful feeling, it arises in his mind. Being contacted by that painful feeling, it is in sensual pleasure that he seeks delight. What is the reason for that? Monks, the uninstructed worldling does not know of any escape from painful feeling other than sensual pleasure. When he delights in sensual pleasure, if in pleasant feeling there is a certain latent disposition toward lust, it arises in his mind. He does not realize as it really is the arising, the passing away, the gratification, the danger, or the escape in the case of those feelings.

Because he does not realize as it really is the arising, the passing away, the gratification, the danger, or the escape in the case of those feelings, if there arises in him a certain latent disposition toward ignorance born of neither-painful-nor-pleasant feeling, that too would

> arise. Then, if he feels a pleasant feeling, he feels it attached to that feeling. If he feels a painful feeling, he feels it attached to that feeling. If he feels a neither-painful-nor-pleasant feeling, he feels it attached to that feeling. Monks, this uninstructed worldling is called one who is attached to birth, aging-and-death, sorrow, lamentation, pain, grief, and despair, one who is attached to suffering.
>
> SN 36.6 – The Dart (Salla Sutta)

It is usually the nature of beings to become deluded by arising feelings. This is because feelings arise influenced by ignorance. When the mind is deluded by a pleasant feeling, all that happens is that one becomes attached to the pleasant feeling. When the mind is deluded by a painful feeling, one then sorrows in the face of painful feeling. When the mind is deluded by a neither-painful-nor-pleasant feeling, one becomes even more deluded. It is amazing how in the face of painful feeling people weep and wail. The Buddha compared this suffering to be like falling into an abyss.

Feeling Is an Abyss

> Monks, the uninstructed worlding makes such a statement: "In the great ocean there is an abyss." Yet, monks, it is about a place that is nowhere to be found and nonexistent that he makes such a statement: "In the great ocean there is an abyss." Monks, "abyss" is a designation for painful bodily feelings. Monks, when the uninstructed worldling comes into contact with a painful feeling, he sorrows, he faints, he laments, he weeps beating his breast, he loses his mind. Monks,

> it is regarding this that it is said: "The uninstructed worldling gains no footing in this abyss, nor does he realize the way to gain a foothold."
>
> SN 36.4 – The Bottomless Abyss (Pātāla Sutta)

There is a cause for weeping and wailing in the face of suffering. There is a cause for infatuation in the face of comfort and happiness. There is a cause for being deluded in the face of neither-painful-nor-pleasant feelings. The Buddha instructed us to eradicate all these causes and be liberated from everything.

Be Wise When Reacting to Feelings

> Monks, there are these three feelings. What three? Pleasant feeling, painful feeling, neither-painful-nor-pleasant feeling. Monks, it is the latent disposition to lust (the lust in the deep recesses of the mind) that should be abandoned in regard to pleasant feeling. In the same way, it is the latent disposition to aversion (the deep-seated anger in the mind) that should be abandoned in regard to painful feeling. It is the latent disposition to ignorance (the deep-seated delusion in the mind) that should be abandoned in regard to neither-painful-nor-pleasant feeling.
>
> If, monks, one day a monk abandons the latent disposition to lust in regard to pleasant feeling, the latent disposition to aversion in regard to painful feeling, and the latent disposition to ignorance in regard to neither-painful-nor-pleasant feeling, then this monk is called one who has abandoned the latent disposition

> to lust, one who has severed craving, one who has gone beyond bonds, one who has perfectly realized conceit and has made an end to all suffering.
>
> SN 36.3 – Abandonment (Pahāna Sutta)

Our journey in saṃsāra, the endless cycle of birth and death, is led astray by feeling. Not only do beings become helpless in the face of feeling, they also become sullied with defilements. The Buddha's instruction to us is to understand this well and eliminate the things that cause saṃsāra to continue. One who is capable of properly directing his wisdom to realize the causes that prolong the journey in saṃsāra can solve this problem.

Realize Feeling as Well

Feeling is related to the first noble truth, which has to be realized. It should be realized that feeling is nonself, that it is subject to the natural law of change. It should also be realized that feeling arises because of contact and ceases with the cessation of contact.

Feeling Is a Water Bubble

> Monks, in the autumn it rains, and thick raindrops fall. Then water bubbles arise on the surface of the water and burst. A man with good sight looks at these water bubbles, ponders them, and investigates them with wisdom. He who looks at these water bubbles, ponders them, and investigates them with wisdom realizes these water bubbles to be void, lowly, and worthless. Truly, monks, what substance is there in a water bubble?
>
> SN 22.95 – A Lump of Foam (Pheṇapiṇḍūpama Sutta)

Investigate All Feelings with Wisdom

So too, monks, whatever kind of feeling there is, whether past, future, or present, internal (what is considered to be oneself) or external, gross or subtle, inferior or superior, far or near: a monk ponders it and investigates it with wisdom.

SN 22.95 – A Lump of Foam (Pheṇapiṇḍūpama Sutta)

The Simile of the Water Bubble

Then to the monk who inspects that feeling, ponders upon that feeling, and investigates it with wisdom, it would appear to be void, lowly, and worthless. Truly, monks, what substance is there in a water bubble?

SN 22.95 – A Lump of Foam (Pheṇapiṇḍūpama Sutta)

These feelings that are pleasant, painful, or neither-painful-nor-pleasant, do not arise without a reason; it is because of contact that they all arise.

And what, monks, is feeling? Monks, there are these six types of feeling: feeling born of eye-contact, feeling born of ear-contact, feeling born of nose-contact, feeling born of tongue-contact, feeling born of body-contact, feeling born of mind-contact. This, monks, is called feeling.

SN 12.2 – Analysis of Dependent Origination (Vibhaṅga Sutta)

Feeling Is Conditioned

Monks, these three feelings are impermanent, conditioned, dependently arisen, subject to disintegration, subject to destruction, of such a nature that one should eradicate attachment toward them, of such a nature that one should cease attaching to them. What three feelings? Pleasant feeling, painful feeling, neither-painful-nor-pleasant feeling. Monks, it is these three feelings that are impermanent, conditioned, dependently arisen, subject to disintegration, subject to destruction, of such a nature that one should eradicate attachment toward them, of such a nature that one should cease attaching to them.

SN 36.9 – Impermanent (Anicca Sutta)

A Dhamma Discussion on Feeling

Then a certain monk approached the Blessed One, paid homage to him, sat down to one side, and said to him: "Here, venerable sir, while I was meditating in seclusion in an inconspicuous place, a thought such as this came to my mind: 'It is of three feelings that the Blessed One has spoken: pleasant feeling, painful feeling, neither-painful-nor-pleasant feeling. It is of these three feelings that the Blessed One has spoken. There is also the fact that the Blessed One has said: "Whatever is felt, that is suffering."' With reference to what did the Blessed One state: 'Whatever is felt, that is suffering?'"

"Good, good, monk! Monk, these three feelings have been stated by me: pleasant feeling, painful feeling, neither-painful-nor-pleasant feeling. These three feelings have been spoken of by me. Monk, there is this fact that has been stated by me: 'Whatever is felt, that is suffering.' Monk, I stated that fact—'Whatever is felt, that is suffering,'—to show the impermanence of formations. Monk, there is this fact that has been stated by me: 'Whatever is felt, that is suffering.' Monk, I stated that fact—'Whatever is felt, that is suffering,'—to show the disintegrating nature of formations … the destructible nature of formations … that formations are of such a nature that one should not be attached to them … that formations are of such a nature that one should cease attaching to them … the changing nature of formations."

SN 36.11 – Alone (Rahogata Sutta)

Is Feeling Previous Kamma?

Some people think that all feelings, pleasant and painful, arise due to previous kamma. They believe that everything happens due to kamma. This is not the teaching of the Buddha.

On one occasion the Blessed One was dwelling at Rājagaha in the Bamboo Grove, the Squirrel Sanctuary. Then the wanderer Moḷiyasīvaka approached the Blessed One and exchanged greetings with him. When they had concluded their greetings and cordial talk, he sat down to one side and said to the Blessed One: "Master Gotama, there are some ascetics and brahmins who hold such a doctrine and view as this: 'Whatever feeling a person experiences, whether it be pleasant or painful or neither-painful-nor-pleasant, all those feelings are the results of one's past kamma.' What does Master Gotama say about this?"

"Some feelings, Sīvaka, arise here originating from bile disorders: if in some way there arise here feelings originating from bile disorders, in this way one should understand for oneself that there arise feelings originating from bile disorders, and that is a known truth in the world, that there arise here some feelings originating from bile disorders."

Overshooting the Norms

"But, Sīvaka, as to that if certain ascetics and brahmins hold such a view and state thus: 'Whatever a person experiences, whether it be pleasant or painful or neither-painful-nor-pleasant, all those feelings are the results of his past kamma.' Then they overshoot what one knows by oneself and they overshoot what is a known truth in the world. Therefore, I say those are false statements on the part of those ascetics and brahmins.

"Some feelings, Sīvaka, arise here originating from phlegm disorders ... arise here originating from air disorders ... arise here originating from an imbalance [of bile, phlegm, and wind] ... arise here originating from change of climate ... arise here originating from undue bodily behavior ... arise here originating from malevolent contrivances ... some feelings, Sīvaka, arise here originating from the results of kamma: if in some way there arise here feelings originating from the results of kamma, in this way one should understand for oneself that there arise feelings originating from the results of kamma, and that is a known truth in the world, that there arise here some feelings originating from the results of kamma. But, Sīvaka, as to that if certain ascetics and brahmins hold such a view and state thus: 'Whatever a person experiences, whether it be pleasant or painful or neither-painful-nor-pleasant, all those feelings are the results of his past kamma.' Then they overshoot what one knows by oneself and they overshoot what is a known truth in the world. Therefore, I say those are false statements on the part of those ascetics and brahmins."

SN 36.21 – Sīvaka (Moḷiyasīvaka Sutta)

Classifications of Feelings

It is the Buddha who investigated feelings by various means. The Buddha's realization of feelings is absolutely amazing. The Buddha classified feelings in one hundred and eight ways.

Monks, I will teach you a Dhamma exposition which includes one hundred and eight means.

Two Kinds of Feelings

And what, monks, are the two kinds of feelings? Bodily feeling and mental feeling. Monks, these are called the two kinds of feelings.

Three Kinds of Feelings

And what, monks, are the three kinds of feelings? Pleasant feeling, painful feeling, neither-painful-nor-pleasant feeling. Monks, these are called the three kinds of feelings.

Five Kinds of Feelings

And what, monks, are the five kinds of feelings? The pleasure faculty, the pain faculty, the joy faculty, the sadness faculty, the equanimity faculty. Monks, these are called the five kinds of feelings.

Six Kinds of Feelings

And what, monks, are the six kinds of feelings? Feeling born of eye-contact, feeling born of ear-contact, feeling born of nose-contact, feeling born of tongue-contact, feeling born of body-contact, feeling born of mind-contact. Monks, these are called the six kinds of feeling.

Eighteen Kinds of Feelings

And what, monks, are the eighteen kinds of feelings? Six classes of feeling associated with joy, six classes of feeling associated with sadness, six classes of feeling associated with equanimity. Monks, these are called the eighteen kinds of feelings.

Thirty-Six Kinds of Feelings

And what, monks, are the thirty-six kinds of feelings? Six feelings of joy associated with the five facets of sensual pleasure, six feelings of joy associated with the renunciation of sensual pleasure; six feelings of sadness associated with the five facets of sensual pleasure, six feelings of sadness associated with the renunciation of sensual pleasure; six feelings of equanimity associated with the five facets of sensual pleasure, six feelings of equanimity associated with the renunciation of sensual pleasure. Monks, these are called the thirty-six kinds of feelings.

One Hundred and Eight Feelings

> And what, monks, are the one hundred and eight kinds of feelings? The [above] thirty-six feelings in the past, the [above] thirty-six feelings in the future, the [above] thirty-six feelings at present. Monks, these are called the one hundred and eight kinds of feelings.
>
> SN 36.22 – The Theme of the Hundred and Eight (Aṭṭhasatapariyāya Sutta)

In this way we can understand the profound meaning contained in the word "feeling" explained by the Buddha in the law of Dependent Origination. We do not experience pleasure or pain due to the will of a creator god. Even devas do not experience pleasure or pain due to the will of a creator god. Feeling is the result of a cause, namely contact. But there were instances when even certain ascetics were baffled by this.

Timbaruka Is Puzzled by Feeling

Once, an ascetic named Timbaruka came to meet the Buddha at Sāvatthi. Having arrived, Timbaruka began questioning the Buddha:

> "How indeed is it, Master Gotama: are pleasure and pain created by oneself?"
>
> "Timbaruka, do not say so," the Blessed One said.
>
> "Then, Master Gotama, are pleasure and pain created by another?"
>
> "Timbaruka, do not say so," the Blessed One said.
>
> "How is it then, Master Gotama: are pleasure and pain created both by oneself and by another?"

"Timbaruka, do not say so," the Blessed One said.

"Then, Master Gotama, have pleasure and pain arisen by chance, being created neither by oneself nor by another?"

"Timbaruka, do not say so," the Blessed One said.

Timbaruka never expected to get these responses from the Buddha. He was flummoxed. Then, he asked the Buddha the following question:

"How is it then, Master Gotama: is there no pleasure and pain?"

"Timbaruka, it is not that there is no pleasure and pain. Timbaruka, there is indeed pleasure and pain."

"Then is it that Master Gotama does not know pleasure and pain? And does not see pleasure and pain?"

"Timbaruka, I am not a person who does not know pleasure and pain. Nor am I a person who does not see pleasure and pain. Timbaruka, truly I know pleasure and pain. I see pleasure and pain."

Eventually Timbaruka became exasperated. The Buddha replied in this manner with the intention of making Timbaruka's mind conducive to understanding the Dhamma. Timbaruka had arrived at the correct line of reasoning. Finally, he appealed to the Buddha thus:

Venerable sir, may the Blessed One explain pleasure and pain to me! May the Blessed One teach me about pleasure and pain!

Then, the Blessed One explained to Timbaruka how beings arrive at wrong views by not understanding the reality of feelings, and how beings free themselves from such wrong views and understand the reality of feelings.

Understanding Life Through Feelings

> Timbaruka, if a person has the initial thought: "That is feeling, he is the one experiencing feeling," he would arrive at the view: "There exist pleasure and pain caused by oneself," I do not say so. A person who experiences feeling with the thought: "Feeling is one thing. The one experiencing feeling is another," he would arrive at the view: "There exist pleasure and pain that had been caused by another," I do not say so.
>
> Timbaruka, without veering toward either of these extremes, the Tathāgata teaches the Dhamma by the Middle Way, which is: "With ignorance as condition, formations come to be; with formations as condition, consciousness comes to be...."
>
> SN 12.18 Timbaruka – (Timbaruka Sutta)

Do Not Be Deluded by Feelings

If one does not understand the reality of feelings, it will not be possible to understand the sublime Dhamma.

> Monks, one may question: "What now is feeling, and to whom does this feeling belong?" Monks, another would say: "Feeling is something else; feeling belongs to someone else." Though expressed in different ways, both of these expressions mean the same thing.

> Monks, if there is the view: "The soul and the body are one," one cannot reap the benefits of the Noble Eightfold Path. So too, monks, if there is the view: "The soul is one thing, the body is another," then again, one cannot reap the benefits of the Noble Eightfold Path. Monks, without arriving at either of these extremes, the Tathāgata teaches the Dhamma by the Middle Way: "With contact as condition, feeling comes to be...."
>
> SN 12.36 – With Ignorance as Condition (2)
> (Dutiya Avijjādī Paccaya Sutta)

From What Do These Feelings Arise?

The Blessed One instructed us that feelings can be observed and understood in various ways. He proclaimed with absolute certainty that feelings are not created by oneself, not created by a god, not created by anyone else, nor do they arise by chance.

Unlike the beings of the world, the devas, Brahmas, ascetics and brahmins, the Buddha was not deluded by, infatuated with, or attached to feelings. He understood the reality of all feelings by gaining true realization that "feeling" is the result of a cause.

He was able to solve extremely complex problems like these due to his skill in investigating and understanding with wisdom.

> When what exists does feeling come to be? By what is feeling conditioned?
>
> SN 12.10 – Gotama the Great Sakyan Sage (Gotama Sutta)

The Buddha once and for all solved this problem that no one else in the world was able to solve.

Feelings Are Caused by Contact

When there is contact, feeling comes to be; feeling has contact as its condition (*phassa paccayā vedanā*).

SN 12.10 – Gotama the Great Sakyan Sage (Gotama Sutta)

I say, monks, that feeling too arises with a cause, not without a cause. And what is the cause for feeling? It should be said—contact.

SN 12.23 – Proximate Cause (Upanisa Sutta)

Chapter 11

Contact

And what, monks, is contact? There are these six kinds of contact: eye-contact, ear-contact, nose-contact, tongue-contact, body-contact, mind-contact. Monks, this is called contact.

SN 12.2 – Analysis of Dependent Origination (Vibhaṅga Sutta)

Feeling Arises from Contact

Monks, these three feelings are born of contact, rooted in contact, and have contact as their source and condition. What three feelings? Pleasant feeling, painful feeling, neither-painful-nor-pleasant feeling.

SN 36.10 – Rooted in Contact (Phassamūlaka Sutta)

Feeling Changes When Contact Changes

Monks, pleasant feeling arises in dependence on contact that brings about pleasant feeling. If there is a pleasant feeling to be experienced—born of contact that brings about pleasant feeling—with the cessation of that very contact which brings about pleasant feeling, that pleasant feeling ceases and subsides.

Monks, painful feeling arises in dependence on contact that brings about painful feeling. If there is a painful feeling to be experienced—born of contact that brings about painful feeling—with the cessation of that very contact which brings about painful feeling, that painful feeling ceases and subsides.

Monks, neither-painful-nor-pleasant feeling arises in dependence on contact that brings about neither-painful-nor-pleasant feeling. If there is a neither-painful-nor-pleasant feeling to be experienced—born of contact that brings about neither-painful-nor-pleasant feeling—with the cessation of that very contact which brings about neither-painful-nor-pleasant feeling, that neither-painful-nor-pleasant feeling ceases and subsides.

SN 36.10 – Rooted in Contact (Phassamūlaka Sutta)

Like Fire

Monks, it is something like this: heat is generated and fire is produced from the conjunction and friction of two sticks. When the same sticks are separated and laid aside the resultant heat ceases and subsides. Monks, in the same way, these three feelings are born of contact, rooted in contact, and have contact as their source and condition. In dependence on the respective contacts the corresponding feelings arise; with the cessation of the respective contacts the corresponding feelings cease.

SN 36.10 – Rooted in Contact (Phassamūlaka Sutta)

Contact Puts You in Contact with Saṃsāra

Contact is completely responsible for shaping life for the continuation of saṃsāra, the cycle of rebirth. With the arising of contact, feeling arises. With the cessation of contact, feeling ceases. This is why no feelings remain unchanged. However, the average person does not know what causes the arising of a feeling. As a result, he or she neither knows the reality of feelings nor their cause. It is essential that we realize that feelings change constantly due to the change of contact.

A Dhamma Discussion on Contact

Once, the Buddha explained contact to Dīghanakha (Aggivessana by clan name), a fire-worshipping ascetic:

> There are, Aggivessana, three kinds of feeling: pleasant feeling, painful feeling, and neither-painful-nor-pleasant feeling. Aggivessana, in an instance where one feels a pleasant feeling, at that moment one does not feel a painful feeling, nor does one feel a neither-painful-nor-pleasant feeling; it is only a pleasant feeling that one feels at that moment. Aggivessana, in an instance where one feels a painful feeling, at that moment one does not feel a pleasant feeling, nor does one feel a neither-painful-nor-pleasant feeling; it is only a painful feeling that one feels at that moment. Aggivessana, in an instance where one feels a neither-painful-nor-pleasant feeling, at that moment one does not feel a pleasant feeling, nor does one feel a painful feeling; it is only a neither-painful-nor-pleasant feeling that one feels at that moment.

Pleasant feeling, Aggivessana, is impermanent, conditioned, dependently arisen, subject to disintegration, subject to destruction, of such a nature that one should eradicate attachment toward it, of such a nature that one should cease attaching to it. Aggivessana, painful feeling, too, is impermanent, conditioned, dependently arisen, subject to disintegration, subject to destruction, of such a nature that one should eradicate attachment toward it, of such a nature that one should cease attaching to it. Aggivessana, neither-painful-nor-pleasant feeling too is impermanent, conditioned, dependently arisen, subject to disintegration, subject to destruction, of such a nature that one should eradicate attachment toward it, of such a nature that one should cease attaching to it.

MN 74 – To Dīghanakha (Dīghanakha Sutta)

The Reality of Contact

Monks, consciousness comes to be in dependence on two. And how, monks, does consciousness come to be in dependence on two? In dependence on the eye and forms there arises eye-consciousness. The eye is impermanent, changing, becoming otherwise. Forms are impermanent, changing, becoming otherwise. Thus, these two are tottering and foundering, impermanent, changing, becoming otherwise. Eye-consciousness is impermanent, changing, becoming otherwise. Whatever caused and conditioned the arising of eye-consciousness, that cause, that condition, too, is impermanent, changing, becoming otherwise.

> How, monks, could eye-consciousness that has arisen in dependence on conditions that are impermanent, be permanent?
>
> Monks, the meeting, the unification, the concurrence of these three things (the eye, forms, and eye-consciousness) is called eye-contact. Eye-contact, too, is impermanent, changing, becoming otherwise. Whatever caused and conditioned the arising of eye-contact, that cause, that condition, too, is impermanent, changing, becoming otherwise. How, monks, could eye-contact that has arisen in dependence on conditions that are impermanent, be permanent? Monks, it is after the arising of contact that one feels. It is after the arising of contact that one perceives. It is after the arising of contact that one thinks thoughts. Thus, these things too are tottering and foundering, impermanent, changing, becoming otherwise.
>
> SN 35.93 – The Dyad (2) (Dutiya Dvaya Sutta)

Now you may have understood what contact is. Contact is not something trivial. Contact occurs in an instant. As soon as contact arises, there also arises feeling, perception, and volition. Contact contributes significantly toward our prolonged existence in saṃsāra. Therefore, the Buddha described contact as a nutriment that nourishes our existence in saṃsāra.

Nutriment for Saṃsāra

> Monks, there are these four nutriments for the existence of beings that have been born and for the assistance of those about to be born. What are those four nutriments?

Edible food, gross or subtle. Second, the nutriment of contact. Third, the nutriment of mental volition. Fourth, the nutriment of consciousness. Monks, these four nutriments support the existence of beings that have been born and act for the assistance of those about to be born.

If, monks, there is lust for the nutriment of contact, if there is desire, if there is craving, consciousness becomes established there and comes to growth. Wherever consciousness becomes established and comes to growth, there is immersion of name-and-form (feeling, perception, volition, contact, mental awareness; the four great elements and the form derived from the four great elements). Where there is immersion of name-and-form, there is the growth of volitional formations (meritorious formations, demeritorious formations, and imperturbable formations). Where there is the growth of volitional formations, there is the production of renewed existence and birth. Where there is the production of renewed existence and birth, there is rebirth and aging-and-death. I say, monks, where there is rebirth and aging-and-death, that is accompanied by much sorrow, anguish, and despair.

SN 12.64 – If There Is Lust (Atthirāga Sutta)

Are Temporary Solutions Enough?

Therefore, lust for contact is a serious problem that results in suffering in saṃsāra. If so, what must we do? Should we temporarily avoid contact by suppressing the awareness of contact through some kind of meditation? Or, should we understand the reality of contact through serenity and insight meditation, eradicate ignorance regarding contact, and be liberated from lust? What is the true solution?

A Permanent Solution

> If, monks, there is no lust for the nutriment of contact, if there is no desire, if there is no craving, consciousness does not become established there and come to growth. Where consciousness does not become established and come to growth, there is no immersion of name-and-form. Where there no is immersion of name-and-form, there is no growth of volitional formations. Where there is no growth of volitional formations, there is no production of renewed existence and birth. Where there is no production of renewed existence and birth, there is no rebirth or aging-and-death. I say, monks, where there is no rebirth or aging-and-death, that is without sorrow, anguish, and despair.

The Beam of Sunlight with No Place to Land

> "Monks, suppose there is a building or a hall with a peaked roof. It has windows either on the northern side, southern side, or the eastern side. When the sun rises and sunbeams enter through a window, where would the beams fall?"
>
> "Venerable sir, the sunbeams would fall on the western wall."
>
> "Monks, if there were no western wall, where would the sunbeams fall?"
>
> "Venerable sir, the sunbeams would fall on the earth."

"Monks, in case there were no earth, where would the sunbeams fall?"

"Venerable sir, on the water."

"Monks, in case there were no water, where would the sunbeams fall?"

"Venerable sir, the sunbeams would not become established anywhere."

"Monks, in the same way, if there is no lust for the nutriment of contact, if there is no desire, if there is no craving, consciousness does not become established there and come to growth. Where consciousness does not become established and come to growth, there is no immersion of name-and-form. Where there no is immersion of name-and-form, there is no growth of volitional formations. Where there is no growth of volitional formations, there is no production of renewed existence and birth. Where there is no production of renewed existence and birth, there is no rebirth or aging-and-death. I say, monks, where there is no rebirth or aging-and-death, that is without sorrow, anguish, and despair."

SN 12.64 – If There Is Lust (Atthirāga Sutta)

The Buddha clearly taught us how the suffering of saṃsāra is renewed due to the desire for contact and how the eradication of desire for contact leads to liberation from the suffering of saṃsāra. He also pointed out a simile which is helpful in realizing the nature of contact.

The Flayed Cow

> Monks, how should the nutriment of contact be seen? Monks, suppose there is a flayed cow. If this cow were leaning against a wall, the creatures dwelling in the wall would nibble at her. If the cow were leaning against a tree, the creatures dwelling in the tree would nibble at her. If the cow were in the water, the creatures dwelling in the water would nibble at her. If the cow were in the open, the creatures dwelling in the open would nibble at her. Monks, whatever the flayed cow exposes herself to, the creatures dwelling there would nibble at her. Monks, it is in such a way that I say the nutriment of contact should be seen.
>
> Monks, if the nutriment of contact is fully realized, the three kinds of feeling are fully realized. If the three kinds of feeling are fully realized, for that noble disciple, I say, there is nothing more to be done for the attainment of Nibbāna.
>
> SN 12.63 – Son's Flesh (Puttamaṃsa Sutta)

Do Not Sidestep the Issue

The above simile clearly shows that the various meditation techniques of the present-day that train one to avoid contact by letting go of the perception of phenomena (forms, sounds, odors, tastes, tangibles, mental phenomena) will not help us to escape from the problem of saṃsāra. It is true that there is a temporary relief in not perceiving phenomena, but by that alone the ignorance and lust associated with contact cannot be eradicated.

These meditation techniques do not result in the cessation of lust for contact. The ignorance and lust regarding contact will be eradicated only when the true nature of contact is realized.

The flayed cow is incapable of escaping from the grasp of the creatures to which she is exposed. In the same way, feeling arises the very instant contact arises.

Investigate Well

The very instant the eye, forms, and eye-consciousness unite, there arises a pleasant feeling, painful feeling, or neither-painful-nor-pleasant feeling.

The very instant the ear, sounds, and ear-consciousness unite, there arises a pleasant feeling, painful feeling, or neither-painful-nor-pleasant feeling.

The very instant the nose, odors, and nose-consciousness unite, there arises a pleasant feeling, painful feeling, or neither-painful-nor-pleasant feeling.

The very instant the tongue, flavors, and tongue-consciousness unite, there arises a pleasant feeling, painful feeling, or neither-painful-nor-pleasant feeling.

The very instant the body, tangibles, and body-consciousness unite, there arises a pleasant feeling, painful feeling, or neither-painful-nor-pleasant feeling.

The very instant the mind, mental phenomena, and mind-consciousness unite, there arises a pleasant feeling, painful feeling, or neither-painful-nor-pleasant feeling.

In whatever feeling that arises, if lust, desire, and craving are present, consciousness is established there and grows.

But, if there is no lust, desire, and craving regarding feeling, consciousness is not established there. As consciousness is not established, it does not grow. For that very reason, one is liberated from consciousness.

It becomes clear to us that contact is always instrumental in creating suffering in saṃsāra because it is a nutriment that nourishes the cycle of rebirth. It is indeed because of contact that there is such a thing as pleasure and pain. Therefore, the disciple should understand this well. Some practitioners follow incorrect meditation techniques and train to attain a state of concentration by non-perception of phenomena, which only temporarily nullifies contact. Thereby, one may be deluded into thinking that one has conquered contact, but in fact, having taken up an incorrect meditation technique, one has been led away from the Noble Eightfold Path. What should be done is to realize the true nature of contact, seeing it as it is. Suffering is something that has to be realized (*pariññeyya*). The reality of contact must be realized in a way that leads to the cessation of ignorance regarding contact and the craving for contact.

See the Truth as Truth

> I have said, Ānanda, that suffering is dependently arisen. What is the cause of suffering? Suffering arises dependent on contact. One who speaks thus is one who states what has indeed been said me. He does not misrepresent me with what is contrary to fact. He is one who speaks in accordance with the Dhamma I have taught. When the Dhamma is stated thus, based

on irrefutable facts, it does not become a target for criticism.

SN 12.25 – Bhūmija (Bhūmija Sutta)

Whatever One Might Say, This is the Truth

Ānanda, even if anyone among those ascetics and brahmins, who are proponents of kamma, states that suffering is caused by oneself—surely none of them would ever experience feeling without contact. Even if anyone among those ascetics and brahmins, who are proponents of kamma, states that suffering is caused by another—surely none of them would ever experience feeling without contact. Even if anyone among those ascetics and brahmins, who are proponents of kamma, states that suffering is caused both by oneself and another—surely none of them would ever experience feeling without contact. Even if anyone among those ascetics and brahmins, who are proponents of kamma, states that suffering is not caused by oneself or by another, but arisen by chance—surely none of them would ever experience feeling without contact.

SN 12.25 – Bhūmija (Bhūmija Sutta)

When What Exists Does Contact Arise?

The Blessed One, the Buddha, had amazing wisdom. The Buddha was the only one who was able to direct his wisdom methodically and scientifically until he understood the reality of life, without becoming attached to, deceived by, or succumbing to any view of the world along the way. He achieved his marvelous realization through what can be considered an extremely modern, scientific experiment, which was to identify the cause of an arisen phenomenon, and then extirpate that very cause.

After discovering the nature of contact, its function, and all other aspects regarding contact, the Buddha then directed his attention to finding out what causes the arising of contact.

> When what exists does contact come to be? By what is contact conditioned?
>
> SN 12.10 – Gotama the Great Sakyan Sage (Gotama Sutta)

The Buddha who was extremely skilled in wise consideration, with his infinite power of wisdom discovered the cause of contact.

> When there are the six sense bases, contact comes to be; contact has the six sense bases as its condition (*saḷāyatana paccayā phasso*).
>
> SN 12.10 – Gotama the Great Sakyan Sage (Gotama Sutta)

Chapter 12

The Six Sense Bases

> Monks, what are the six sense bases? The eye base, the ear base, the nose base, the tongue base, the body base, the mind base. Monks, these are called the six sense bases.
>
> SN 12.2 – Analysis of Dependent Origination (Vibhaṅga Sutta)

A Dhamma Discussion on the Six Sense Bases

Once, the Venerable Sāriputta explained a discourse taught by the Buddha on happiness and suffering to a group of followers of other religious sects. The Venerable Ānanda, who overheard this Dhamma discussion, told the Blessed One about it. Then the Buddha, rejoicing in venerable Ānanda's narrative, explained that all the suffering in the world arises due to contact. Delighted with the Buddha's words, the Venerable Ānanda said:

> Venerable sir, it is wonderful! Venerable sir, it is amazing! How the entire meaning can be stated by a single word (contact)! Venerable sir, when the same meaning is stated in detail, will not a deeper meaning be revealed? Will not a deeper understanding arise?

Then, the Blessed One instructed venerable Ānanda on how to understand the matter in greater detail. The Venerable Ānanda continued:

> Venerable sir, if they were to ask me: "Venerable friend Ānanda, what is the origin of contact? What is the arising of contact, from what is contact born? What is the source of contact?" Then, venerable sir, I would answer that question in this way: "Dear friends, the origin of contact is the six sense bases. Contact arises from the six sense bases; contact is born from the six sense bases; contact has the six sense bases as its source."
>
> "Venerable friends, with the complete cessation of the six sense bases, contact ceases."
>
> SN 12.24 – Wanderers of Other Sects (Aññatitthiya Sutta)

The cessation of the six sense bases of contact means the cessation of craving toward the six senses—the eye, ear, nose, tongue, body, and mind. It does not mean losing one's awareness of the six senses.

Recognize the Six Sense Bases

The Buddha clearly pointed out that one must understand the six sense bases just as they really are.

> Monks, the eye is impermanent. Whatever is impermanent, that is suffering. Whatever is suffering, that is nonself (i.e., one cannot exercise control over it). Whatever is nonself should be seen as it really is with developed wisdom thus: "This is not mine, this I am not, this is not my self."

The ear is impermanent.... The nose is impermanent.... The tongue is impermanent.... The body is impermanent.... The mind is impermanent. Whatever is impermanent, that is suffering. Whatever is suffering, that is nonself (one cannot exercise control over it). Whatever is nonself should be seen as it really is with developed wisdom thus: "This is not mine, this I am not, this is not my self."

SN 35.1 – The Internal as Impermanent
(Ajjhattānicca Sutta)

This Is the Reality

The Blessed One performed a comprehensive research on the six sense bases. He describes the noble research he carried out via serenity and insight meditation in the following way:

Monks, before my Enlightenment, while I was still a Bodhisatta [in this life], not yet fully enlightened, it occurred to me: "What is the gratification, what is the danger, what is the escape in the case of the eye? ... in the case of the ear ... in the case of the nose ... in the case of the tongue ... in the case of the body ... What is the gratification, what is the danger, what is the escape in the case of the mind?"

Then, monks, it occurred to me: "The pleasure and joy that arise in dependence on the eye: this is the gratification in the eye. That the eye is impermanent, suffering, and subject to change: this is the danger in the eye. The elimination and eradication of desire and lust for the eye—this is the escape from the eye."

"The pleasure and joy that arise in dependence on the ear ... the nose ... the tongue ... the body ... the mind: this is the gratification in the mind. That the mind is impermanent, suffering, and subject to change: this is the danger in the mind. The elimination and eradication of desire and lust for the mind—this is the escape from the mind."

SN 35.13 – Before My Enlightenment (Sambodha Sutta)

Enamored with the Gratification

Monks, if there were no gratification in the eye, beings would not become enamored with it. Monks, due to certain reasons there is gratification in the eye, that is why beings become enamored with the eye.

Experiencing Revulsion Due to the Danger

Monks, if there were no danger in the eye, beings would not experience revulsion toward it. Monks, due to certain reasons there is danger in the eye, that is why beings having understood the true nature of the eye experience revulsion toward the eye.

Escape by Eradicating Desire

Monks, if there were not an escape from the eye, beings would not escape from the eye. Monks, due to certain reasons there is an escape from the eye, that is why beings escape from the eye.

(The same permutations of gratification, danger, and escape apply to the other five sense bases as well.)

Monks, as long as beings have not realized as it really is the gratification as gratification, the danger as danger and the escape as escape with regard to these six internal sense bases, they have not lived separated, detached, or freed from this world with its devas, Māra, and Brahmas, ascetics and brahmins, its population of devas and humans.

SN 35.17 – If There Were No (1) (No Ce Assāda Sutta)

Embracing the Sense Bases Is Embracing Suffering

Monks, if one happily embraces the eye, one happily embraces suffering. And if one happily embraces suffering, I say that one is not free from suffering. Monks, if one happily embraces the ear … the nose … the tongue … the body … Monks, if one happily embraces the mind, one happily embraces suffering. And if one happily embraces suffering, I say that one is not free from suffering.

Rejecting the Sense Bases Is Rejecting Suffering

Monks, if one does not happily embrace the eye, one does not happily embrace suffering. And if one does not happily embrace suffering, I say that one is free from suffering. Monks, if one does not happily embrace the ear … the nose … the tongue … the body … Monks, if one does not happily embrace the mind, one does not happily embrace suffering. And if one does not happily embrace suffering, I say that one is free from suffering.

SN 35.19 – Delight (1) (Abhinanda Sutta)

The Arising of Suffering

> Monks, if there is a birth, existence, specific birth, manifestation, of the eye, that is the arising of suffering, the persistence of disease, the manifestation of aging-and-death. Monks, if there is a birth of the ear … the nose … the tongue … the body … Monks, if there is a birth, existence, specific birth, manifestation, of the mind, that is the arising of suffering, the persistence of disease, the manifestation of aging-and-death.

SN 35.21 – Arising of Suffering (1) (Uppāda Sutta)

Gaining True Knowledge

Once, a monk approached the Buddha and asked him a question:

> "Venerable sir, when one knows in which way, sees in which way, is ignorance eradicated and true knowledge arisen?"
>
> "Monk, it is when one knows and sees the eye as impermanent that ignorance is eradicated and true knowledge (*vijjā*) arisen. It is when one knows and sees forms as impermanent that ignorance is eradicated and true knowledge arisen. It is when one knows and sees eye-consciousness as impermanent that ignorance is eradicated and true knowledge arisen. It is when one knows and sees eye-contact as impermanent that ignorance is eradicated and true knowledge arisen. It is when one knows and sees feelings born of eye-contact—whether pleasant, painful, or neither-painful-nor-pleasant—as impermanent that ignorance is

eradicated and true knowledge arisen. It is when one knows and sees the ear ... nose ... tongue ... body ... mind as impermanent that ignorance is eradicated and true knowledge arisen. It is when one knows and sees mental phenomena as impermanent that ignorance is eradicated and true knowledge arisen. It is when one knows and sees mind-consciousness as impermanent that ignorance is eradicated and true knowledge arisen. It is when one knows and sees mind-contact as impermanent that ignorance is eradicated and true knowledge arisen. It is when one knows and sees feelings born of mind-contact—whether pleasant, painful, or neither-painful-nor-pleasant—as impermanent that ignorance is eradicated and true knowledge arisen."

SN 35.53 – Abandoning Ignorance (Avijjāpahāna Sutta)

Now, we can see how far these six sense bases—the eye, ear, nose, tongue, body, and mind—carry beings in saṃsāra. The day we eradicate craving toward these six sense bases, we too can escape from suffering. As long as craving toward these six sense bases exists, we have to live in suffering.

Do Not Be Deceived

These six sense bases do not arise due to the will of a so-called creator god. Even if a being is referred to as a god, that god has the same impermanent eye, ear, nose, tongue, body, and mind like everyone else. That god is also not free from suffering. That god too, is devoid of a self and is born of the principle of cause and effect. The existence of an everlasting life or a permanent soul is not a possibility. Even for that god too, the only way to escape from suffering is by following the Noble Eightfold Path shown by the Buddha.

Keep Developing Wisdom!

Therefore, we should leave no room in our mind for blind faith and instead learn to investigate with wisdom. We should be wise in understanding that the six sense bases—eye, ear, nose, tongue, body, and mind—are not formed according to one's own wish. Neither are they formed according to someone else's wish, nor have they arisen spontaneously. If such were the case, there would be nothing we could do but to patiently endure.

If these six sense bases were formed according to one's own fancy, no one would fashion for themselves ugly eyes and ears, crippled limbs, or deformed bodies. No one relishes having a mind engulfed in pain and sadness. Does not everyone wish for a life free from sickness, distress, suffering, and turmoil?

There is no one in this world capable of concealing the Buddha's amazing realization about the reality of life. All of the Buddha's effort, mindfulness, concentration, and wisdom were directed toward understanding life.

Of What Are These Six Sense Bases Made?

The beings of the world, having succumbed to the six sense bases, do not think even for a moment about what caused the arising of the sense bases. They have no time to think about it. Often, they are preoccupied with thoughts of enjoyment and gratification of the senses—thoughts about forms, sounds, odors, flavors, tangibles, and mental phenomena, each cognizable by their respective internal sense bases, and the gratification derived therefrom. However, the Buddha did not succumb to the senses. He began investigating the root cause for the arising of the six sense bases.

The Six Sense Bases Are Made of Name-and-Form

> When what exists do the six sense bases come to be? By what are the six sense bases conditioned?

The Buddha found the correct answer as to how the six senses come to be.

> When there is name-and-form, the six sense bases come to be; the six sense bases have name-and-form as their condition (*nāmarūpa paccayā saḷāyatanaṃ*).
>
> SN 12.10 – Gotama the Great Sakyan Sage (Gotama Sutta)

Chapter 13

Name-and-Form

In general, people are accustomed to giving various meanings for name-and-form (*nāmarūpa*). Such understandings are mostly based on their own fanciful interpretations. As a result, we lose the opportunity to understand what the Buddha explained as name-and-form.

In describing name-and-form, some people explain that name refers to the mind and form refers to the body. But it is clearly stated in the Dhamma that mind and body are not subsumed under the classification of name-and-form, rather, they are designated as two of the six sense bases, which originate from name-and-form.

Still others explain name-and-form by dividing the five aggregates of clinging in two. They state that name consists of four aggregates—feeling, perception, volitional formations, and consciousness—and form consists of the form aggregate. However, it is not possible to find such an interpretation of name-and-form in the Dhamma: the Buddha did not include consciousness as a component of name.

What the Buddha really meant by name-and-form can only be understood by studying the discourses of the Buddha.

Understand Name-and-Form

> And what, monks, is name-and-form? Feeling, perception, volition, contact, mental awareness (*vedanā, saññā, cetanā, phassa, manasikāra*): this is called name. The four great elements and the form derived from the four great elements (*cattāro ca mahābhūtā, catunnañca mahābhūtānaṃ upādāyarūpaṃ*): this is called form. Thus, monks, this name and this form are together called name-and-form.
>
> SN 12.2 – Analysis of Dependent Origination (Vibhaṅga Sutta)

Understand Properly

Let us try to understand properly how the Buddha explained name-and-form. He mentioned five things as components of name: feeling, perception, volition, contact, and mental awareness. He referred to the four great elements and all things made up of the four great elements as form.

The Buddha has taught in many ways about mind and body and the five aggregates of clinging. The Buddha did not describe them as name-and-form. The Buddha's discourses on the mind and body must be understood strictly in terms of the mind and body. It is important not to use the terms name-and-form in relation to the mind and body. When discussing the five aggregates of clinging, it is imperative to understand them without dividing them in two as name-and-form.

Clarifying Name-and-Form

Now we know the five things the Buddha explained as name—feeling, perception, volition, contact, and mental awareness.

He has clearly explained that the first three of these—feeling, perception, and volition—arise due to contact. In this way, we can conclude that the Buddha mentioned contact as the fourth component because contact causes the arising of the first three. We can understand from the following discourse that mental awareness is placed in the fifth position because it gives rise to all the other components of name.

The Nature of Mental Awareness

The following is a Dhamma discussion between the Marshal of the Dhamma, venerable Sāriputta, and other monks.

> Venerable friends, if one's eye is intact and no external forms are within the eye's range, and there is no corresponding mental awareness, then there is no manifestation of the corresponding consciousness.
>
> Venerable friends, if one's eye is intact and external forms are within the eye's range, yet if there is no corresponding mental awareness, then there is no manifestation of the corresponding consciousness.
>
> Venerable friends, if one's eye is intact and external forms are within the eye's range, and there is the corresponding mental awareness, then there is the manifestation of the corresponding consciousness.
>
> (The same should be understood regarding the ear, nose, tongue, body, and mind.)
>
> MN 28 – The Greater Discourse on the Simile of the Elephant's Footprint (Mahāhatthipadopama Sutta)

Now we can understand that "mental awareness" (*manasikāra*) is a powerful contributor toward the arising of consciousness. When there is no mental awareness, there is no arising of consciousness. When there is no arising of consciousness, how could there be any contact at all? When there is no contact, how could there be feeling, perception and volition? Therefore, mental awareness is the crucial factor inducing the arising of the other mental phenomena.

The six sense bases together with vitality and warmth exist because of name-and-form. Wherever beings take birth, these six sense bases arise; they arise because of name-and-form, not due to any miracles.

A Unique Analysis of Name-and-Form

The *Mahanidāna Sutta* contains an incredibly profound analysis of name-and-form. In this discourse, the Buddha analyzes name-and-form in a special way. Generally, we have learned that contact arises with the sense bases as condition, and that the sense bases arise due to name-and-form.

Interestingly, in the *Mahanidāna Sutta*, the Buddha, the Lord of the Dhamma, without speaking of the six senses, directly states that contact arises due to name-and-form. He uses the word "contact" in this explanation in order to show the close interrelationship between name-and-form. The Buddha emphasized that the world as we relate to it is entirely based on the union of name-and-form. The Buddha taught us that there are two kinds of contact related to the union of name-and-form.

These two kinds of contact are:

1. Designation-contact of form (*rūpakāye-adhivacanasamphasso*)
2. Impingement-contact of name (*nāmakāye-paṭighasamphasso*)

What Is Designation-Contact of Form (*Rūpa*)?

We already know that form is the four great elements and all things made up of the four great elements.

We identify and talk about all things that are of form by way of established conventions and usage, which are ultimately concepts originating in the mind. This means our experience of form is shaped with feeling, perception, volition, contact, and mental awareness as the basis.

What Is Impingement-Contact of Name (*Nāma*)?

This, too, should be understood with great patience. Name (*nāma*) consists of feeling, perception, volition, contact, and mental awareness. If one talks about something in terms of name (*nāma*), it would be about the four great elements or something made up of the four great elements. In the Dhamma, this is called "impingement-contact of name."

Therefore, nothing exists in the world without designation-contact of form and impingement-contact of name. The interrelation of name-and-form is that subtle.

Designation-Contact of Form

The Blessed One revealed this wonderful interrelation of name-and-form to venerable Ānanda in this way:

"It was said: 'With name-and-form as condition there is contact.'"

"How that is so, Ānanda, should be understood in this way: when name is designated via certain ways, features, signs, and descriptions, in the absence of those ways, features, signs, and descriptions, would there be the designation of form in terms of name?"

"Certainly not, venerable sir."

Impingement-Contact of Name

"When form is designated via certain ways, features, signs, and descriptions, in the absence of those ways, features, signs, and descriptions, would there be the designation of name via impingement-contact?"

"Certainly not, venerable sir."

If Expression via Name-and-Form Were Absent

"Ānanda, when there is the designation of the form enity (*rūpakāya*) and the name entity (*nāmakāya*) via certain ways, features, signs, and descriptions, in the absence of those ways, features, signs, and descriptions, would there be either the designation of form in terms of name (*rūpakāye adhivacanasamphasso*) or the designation of name via impingement-contact (*nāmakāye paṭighasamphasso*)?"

"Certainly not, venerable sir."

There Would Be No Contact

"Ānanda, when there is the designation of the form entity and the name entity via certain ways, features, signs, and descriptions, in the absence of those ways, features, signs, and descriptions, would there be contact?"

"Certainly not, venerable sir."

DN 15 – The Great Discourse on Causation
(Mahānidāna Sutta)

From this profound explanation, we can understand the powerful influence name-and-form has on the continuous formation of saṃsāra. The problem of life is the union and coexistence of name-and-form, both of which are impermanent.

It is when we expand our knowledge through the teachings of the Buddha that we realize how immature is the general understanding of mind as name and body as form.

The Product of Name-and-Form

In conclusion, one's eye arises dependent on name-and-form that is impermanent. One's ear arises dependent on name-and-form that is impermanent. One's nose arises dependent on name-and-form that is impermanent. One's tongue arises dependent on name-and-form that is impermanent. One's body arises dependent on name-and-form that is impermanent. One's mind arises dependent on name-and-form that is impermanent.

How could one's eye, ear, nose, tongue, body, and mind be permanent when they have dependently arisen from impermanent name-and-form?

What Conditions Name-and-Form?

The Buddha had the amazing ability of directing his peerless wisdom in a precise manner. Through his supermundane research, he was gradually resolving the problem of how to permanently liberate life from aging-and-death. After successfully understanding the true nature of the principle of cause and effect all the way up to name-and-form, he began investigating the cause of name-and-form as well.

Consciousness Conditions Name-and-Form

> When what exists does name-and-form come to be? By what is name-and-form conditioned?

The Buddha found the answer. There was nothing hidden from his amazing wisdom.

> When there is consciousness, name-and-form comes to be; name-and-form has consciousness as its condition (*viññāṇa paccayā nāmarūpaṃ*).
>
> SN 12.10 – Gotama the Great Sakyan Sage (Gotama Sutta)

Chapter 14

Consciousness

> Monks, what is consciousness? Monks, there are six classes of consciousness: consciousness which arises in the eye, consciousness which arises in the ear, consciousness which arises in the nose, consciousness which arises in the tongue, consciousness which arises in the body, and consciousness which arises in the mind.
>
> SN 12.2 – Analysis of Dependent Origination (Vibhaṅga Sutta)

Do Not Be Deceived by Consciousness

Though many speak of consciousness, they fail to understand consciousness. When questioned as to what consciousness is, people proffer various views and opinions. When we hear these manifold misconceptions, we understand that many are unaware of the true nature of consciousness. Some say that the Buddha's consciousness is floating in the sky. Others say that the consciousness of the Enlightened Ones goes to infinity. While some believe that even flora has consciousness. It is apparent from these statements that most do not have the slightest idea regarding the nature of consciousness.

Consciousness

Monks, why is it called consciousness? Monks, it "specifically identifies," with this meaning it is called consciousness.

SN 22.79 – Being Devoured (Khajjanīya Sutta)

Understand Consciousness

In many ways I have stated that consciousness is dependently arisen; consciousness does not arise without a cause....

Monks, consciousness is designated by the particular condition dependent upon which it arises. When consciousness arises dependent on the eye and forms, it is designated as eye-consciousness; when consciousness arises dependent on the ear and sounds, it is designated as ear-consciousness; when consciousness arises dependent on the nose and odors, it is designated as nose-consciousness; when consciousness arises dependent on the tongue and flavors, it is designated as tongue-consciousness; when consciousness arises dependent on the body and tangibles, it is designated as body-consciousness; when consciousness arises dependent on the mind and mental phenomena, it is designated as mind-consciousness.

MN 38 – The Greater Discourse on the Destruction of Craving (Mahātaṇhāsankhaya Sutta)

Classifying Fire

Monks, it is something like this. Just as fire is designated by the particular condition dependent on which it burns—if fire burns dependent on logs, it is called a log fire; if fire burns dependent on pieces of wood, it is called a wood fire; if fire burns dependent on grass, it is called a grass fire; if fire burns dependent on cowdung, it is called a cowdung fire; if fire burns dependent on chaff, it called a chaff fire; if fire burns dependent on rubbish, it is called a rubbish fire—so too, consciousness is designated by the particular condition dependent on which it arises.

MN 38 – The Greater Discourse on the Destruction of Craving (Mahātaṇhāsankhaya Sutta)

In the teachings of the Buddha there are these three terms: mind, mentality, and consciousness. There is an instance where all three of these terms are found in the same discourse.

Mind, Mentality, and Consciousness

But, monks, as to that which is called "mind" (*citta*) and "mentality" (*mano*) and "consciousness" (*viññāṇa*)—the uninstructed worldling is unable to experience revulsion toward it, unable to become dispassionate toward it and unable to think of being freed from it. What is the reason for that? Because, monks, for a long time this has been held to by him, appropriated, and grasped thus: "This is mine, this I am, this is my self." Monks, that is why the uninstructed worldling is unable to experience revulsion toward it, unable to become dispassionate toward it and unable to think of being freed from it.

> Monks, if the uninstructed worlding really wanted to consider something as self, it would be better to consider the body made up of the four great elements as such, but it is not proper to consider the mind as such. What is the reason for that? Monks, this body that is made up of the four great elements is to be seen existing for one year, for two years, for three, four, five, or ten years, for twenty, thirty, forty, or fifty years, for a hundred years, or for more than a hundred years.

Changing Rapidly

> But that which is called "mind" and "mentality" and "consciousness" arises as one thing and ceases as another by day and by night.

> Monks, it is something like this. Think of a monkey roaming in a great forest. When that monkey roams in the forest, it grabs hold of a branch, then it lets go of that branch and grabs another, and then lets go of that branch and grabs onto yet another branch. So too, monks, that which is called "mind" and "mentality" and "consciousness" arises as one thing and ceases as another by day and by night.
>
> SN 12.61 – Uninstructed (Assutavantu Sutta)

Mind (*Mano*) Arises from Name-and-Form

The Buddha pointed out that the mind (*mano*) originates from name-and-form. When the Buddha stated, "With name-and-form as condition, the six sense bases come to be (*nāmarūpa paccayā saḷāyatanaṃ*)," here the mind is also included in the six sense bases.

Consciousness Arises from Name-and-Form

Dependent on what does consciousness arise?

> With the arising of name-and-form there is the arising of consciousness. With the cessation of name-and-form there is the cessation of consciousness.
>
> SN 22.57 – The Seven Cases (Sattaṭṭhāna Sutta)

Mind (*Citta*) Arises from Name-and-Form

> With the origination of name-and-form there is the origination of mind (*citta*). With the cessation of name-and-form there is the cessation of mind.
>
> SN 47.42 – Origination (Samudaya Sutta)

Therefore, we should clearly understand that which is called "mind" (*citta*), "mentality" (*mano*), and "consciousness" (*viññāṇa*) are of the nature that they arise conditioned by name-and-form, and cease with the concomitant cessation of name-and-form.

Once the Venerable Mahā Koṭṭhita asked the Venerable Sāriputta:

> How is it, venerable friend Sāriputta: Is consciousness created by oneself? Or is consciousness created by another? Or is consciousness created both by oneself and by another? Or has consciousness arisen by chance, being created neither by oneself nor by another?

Then, the Venerable Sāriputta replied that name-and-form is the cause for the arising of consciousness.

Venerable Mahā Koṭṭhita then asked another question:

> How is it, venerable friend Sāriputta: Is name-and-form created by oneself? Or is name-and-form created by another? Or is name-and-form created both by oneself and by another? Or has name-and-form arisen by chance, being created neither by oneself nor by another?

to which venerable Sāriputta answered that name-and-form arises with consciousness as condition.

Two Bundles of Reeds Leaning against Each Other

When Arahant Mahā Koṭṭhita asked for further clarification from venerable Sāriputta as to the interrelation of consciousness and name-and-form, venerable Sāriputta explained by way of a simile:

> Well then, venerable friend, I will tell you a simile about this. As in this case, even by a simile an intelligent person can understand the meaning of a statement.
>
> Venerable friend, imagine there are two sheaves of reeds left leaning against each other. Venerable friend, it is in the same way that consciousness exists with name-and-form as condition, and name-and-form exists with consciousness as condition. With name-and-form as condition, the six sense bases come to be; with the six sense bases as condition, contact comes to be .... It is in this way that the whole mass of suffering comes to be.

If You Remove One, the Other Would Fall

> Venerable friend, the moment one of those two sheaves of reeds is removed, the other falls, and if the other

sheaf is removed, the first falls.

Venerable friend, it is in the same way that, with the cessation of name-and-form, consciousness ceases; and with the cessation of consciousness, name-and-form ceases. With the cessation of name-and-form, the six sense bases cease; with the cessation of the six sense bases, contact ceases .... It is in this way that the whole mass of suffering ceases.

SN 12.67 – The Sheaves of Reeds (Naḷakaḷāpa Sutta)

Wise Consideration

Wise consideration is the principal quality a disciple should possess in order to realize the Dhamma taught by the Blessed One. It is through wise consideration that one can develop knowledge of things as they really are (*yathābhūta ñāṇa*). The other main supporting factor for gaining yathābhūta ñāṇa is concentration (*samādhi*).

One who wishes to dive to the bottom of the ocean needs a diving suit equipped with an oxygen tank. When he returns to the shore and describes the details about the bottom of the ocean, someone who hears about it may want to experience it as well. That person must also dive to the bottom of the ocean using similar equipment to experience firsthand what he has heard, so that he may decide for himself whether it is true or untrue.

However, without making any effort whatsoever, if someone says it is not possible to dive to the bottom of the ocean, and that there is nothing there as described, such a person is not being truthful. He is merely a person who speaks drivel just because he has a mouth. He would only be displaying his foolishness and stubbornness.

Similarly, in order to understand the truth revealed by the Buddha, one must follow the path shown by him. It is essential to develop virtue, restraint of the sense faculties, wise consideration, and concentration to realize that lofty goal.

Trees Come to Be Because of Seeds

Trees grow from seeds. And upon fruiting, trees produce more seeds. However, if a tree is uprooted completely without leaving even a small root, cut into small pieces, dried, burned, and the ashes winnowed in the wind, the possibility of new seeds developing from that particular tree is eliminated. In short, the tree itself is destroyed. Effects arisen due to causes have the same nature. When causes arise, they give rise to effects. When the causes are eliminated, the effects arisen from those causes are eliminated as well; when the causes are destroyed, the effects arisen from those causes are also destroyed.

It is in the same manner that we should learn the law of Dependent Origination taught by the Buddha. There are instances where the whole of Dependent Origination is described in a nutshell as the five aggregates of clinging, so it should in these instances be learned not in terms of Dependent Origination, but in terms of the five aggregates of clinging. The Buddha is our teacher, the Lord of the Dhamma; we are his disciples. Therefore, when investigating with wisdom, disciples should use the ways and means shown by the Buddha and refrain from using other arbitrary means.

What Conditions Consciousness?

In explaining the process of Dependent Origination, the Buddha teaches that formations (*saṅkhārā*) are the cause for the arising of consciousness. We must try to understand this in the same manner that the Buddha teaches us.

> When what exists does consciousness come to be? By what is consciousness conditioned? ... When there are formations, consciousness comes to be; consciousness has formations as its condition (*saṅkhāra paccayā viññāṇaṃ*).
>
> SN 12.10 – Gotama the Great Sakyan Sage (Gotama Sutta)

Chapter 15

Formations

We should know that the word formations (*saṅkhārā*) carries different meanings in the Dhamma. When explaining the five aggregates of clinging, too, the Buddha uses the word saṅkhārā.

Saṅkhārā within the Five Aggregates of Clinging Are Different

> And what, monks, are volitional formations (*saṅkhārā*)? Monks, there are these six classes of volition: volition regarding forms, volition regarding sounds, volition regarding odors, volition regarding flavors, volition regarding tangibles, volition regarding mental phenomena. Monks, these are called saṅkhārā. With the arising of contact there is the arising of saṅkhārā. With the cessation of contact there is the cessation of saṅkhārā.
>
> SN 22.56 – Phases of the Clinging Aggregates
> (Upādāna Parivatta Sutta)

Here, the word saṅkhārā has clearly been given the meaning of volition, or intention. This volition, too, is affected by ignorance. There is a clear difference between the meaning of saṅkhārā mentioned in the context of the five aggregates of clinging, and the meaning of saṅkhārā mentioned in the law of Dependent Origination. First, let us understand the meaning of saṅkhārā, described as volition, in the context of the five aggregates of clinging.

Here, the essence of volition is its role in perpetuating bhava, the arranging of kamma to bear fruit in future existences in saṃsāra. Hence, re-construction of the five aggregates of clinging occurs again and again. The Buddha described this process as "constructing the conditioned (*abhisaṅkaroti*)."

Saṅkhārā Construct Conditioned Things

> And why, monks, are they called saṅkhārā? Monks, "a thing conditioned by the principle of cause and effect (*saṅkhata*) is specifically constructed to again form a similar thing [which is also conditioned by the principle of cause and effect] (*abhisaṅkaroti*)"—that is why they are called saṅkhārā.
>
> And what thing, conditioned by the principle of cause and effect, is specifically constructed?
>
> Monks, conditioned form is specifically constructed as form; conditioned feeling is specifically constructed as feeling; conditioned perception is specifically constructed as perception; conditioned volitional formations are specifically constructed as volitional formations; conditioned consciousness is specifically constructed as consciousness. Monks, "a thing conditioned by the principle of cause and effect (*saṅkhata*) is specifically constructed to again form a

similar thing [which is also conditioned by the principle of cause and effect] (*abhisaṅkaroti*)"—that is why they are called saṅkhārā.

SN 22.79 – Being Devoured (Khajjanīya Sutta)

A conditioned thing (*saṅkhata*) is described by the Buddha as something in which an arising is to be seen, a cessation is to be seen, and change during its existence is to be seen. The five aggregates of clinging—form, feeling, perception, volitional formations (*saṅkhārā*), and consciousness—have this nature. Therefore, they are described as conditioned things (*saṅkhata*). As saṅkhārā construct conditioned things over and over again, the word saṅkhārā is defined as follows: "A conditioned thing is constructed to create another conditioned thing (*saṅkhatabhisaṅkaronti*)."

The Volitional Formations of the Ignorant Individual

There is another discourse that echoes a similar idea:

> Monks, if a person immersed in ignorance accrues a meritorious volitional formation (i.e., good kamma), his consciousness is formed based on that merit. If he accrues a demeritorious volitional formation (i.e., bad kamma), his consciousness is formed based on that demerit. If he accrues an imperturbable volitional formation (i.e., kamma accrued when dwelling in form and formless jhāna states), his consciousness is formed based on that imperturbable volitional formation.

SN 12.51 – Thorough Investigation (Parivīmaṃsana Sutta)

Another Usage of the Term Saṅkhārā

There is yet another place where the Buddha uses the term saṅkhārā.

> Monks, when realized in what way, when seen in what way, are the taints destroyed in this very life? Here, monks, there is an uninstructed worldling; he is one who does not see noble ones, one who is unskilled in the noble ones' Dhamma, and one who is undisciplined in the noble ones' Dhamma. He is one who does not see exalted persons, one who is unskilled in the Dhamma of exalted persons, and one who is undisciplined in the Dhamma of exalted persons. Deluded, he regards form as self. Monks, that deluded regarding of his is a formation. That formation—what is its origin? From what does it arise? From what is it born? What is its source? Monks, craving has arisen for the uninstructed worldling experiencing a feeling born of contact affected by ignorance. It is from that craving that that formation arises.
>
> But, monks, that formation is impermanent, a thing conditioned by the principle of cause and effect, dependently arisen. That craving, too, is impermanent, a thing conditioned by the principle of cause and effect, dependently arisen. That feeling is impermanent, a thing conditioned by the principle of cause and effect, dependently arisen. That contact is impermanent, a thing conditioned by the principle of cause and effect, dependently arisen. That ignorance is impermanent, a thing conditioned by the principle of cause and effect,

> dependently arisen. Monks, when one realizes in this way, sees in this way, the taints are destroyed in this very life.
>
> SN 22.81 – Pārileyya (Pārileyyaka Sutta)

The Destruction of Volitional Formations

In the above discourses, it is the volition affected by ignorance which re-constructs the same conditioned things (*saṅkhata*) discussed before—form, feeling, perception, volitional formations, and consciousness—that process is described as saṅkhārā.

The Lord of the Dhamma, the Buddha, uttered an inspired utterance (*udāna*) about the cessation of volitional formations: "My mind has reached the destruction of volitional formations; I have attained the destruction of craving (*visaṅkhāragataṃ cittaṃ, taṇhānaṃ khayamajjhagā*)." What is described here is the liberation of the mind from its tendency to re-create existence in saṃsāra. Some misinterpret this by thinking mind (*citta*) to be an unconditioned thing rather than a conditioned thing, and thereby arrive at the eternalist view (*sassata diṭṭhi*). Unknowingly, they are all going in circles trapped in their own view of self. But in reality, liberation of the mind means none other than to escape from craving itself.

The Liberated Mind

The Venerable Mahākaccāna provided a wonderful explanation of the mind liberated from craving to the householder Hāliddikāni.

> Householder, through the destruction, fading away, cessation, giving up, and relinquishment of desire, lust,

> delight, craving, engrossment and clinging, mental standpoints, adherences, and latent dispositions toward the form element, the mind is said to be well liberated.
>
> Householder, if in a person there is desire, lust, delight, craving, engrossment and clinging, mental standpoints, adherences, and latent dispositions toward the form element, with the cessation of those [defilements], with the elimination of attachment, with the cessation of craving, with the abandoning of desire, the mind that has completely eradicated desire is said to be well liberated from those defilements.
>
> SN 22.4 – Hāliddakāni (Dutiya Hāliddikāni Sutta)

This concludes the description of saṅkhārā in the context of the five aggregates of clinging. We should not confuse the definition of saṅkhārā explained in the context of the five aggregates of clinging with that of saṅkhārā explained in the context of the law of Dependent Origination.

Learning Saṅkhārā in the Context of the Law of Dependent Origination

The Buddha explains the meaning of the formations (*saṅkhārā*) mentioned in the law of Dependent Origination.

> Monks, what are known as formations (*saṅkhārā*)? Monks, these formations are threefold: the bodily formation (*kāya saṅkhāra*), the verbal formation (*vacī saṅkhāra*), and the mental formation (*citta saṅkhāra*). These, monks, are called formations.
>
> SN 12.2 – Analysis of Dependent Origination (Vibhaṅga Sutta)

There is a clear explanation about these formations in the *Cūḷavedalla Sutta* of the Majjhima Nikāya.

In-Breathing and Out-Breathing, Applied Thought and Sustained Thought, Perception and Feeling

(Question) "Noble lady, what is the bodily formation? What is the verbal formation? What is the mental formation?"

(Answer) "Friend Visākha, in-breathing and out-breathing are the bodily formation; applied thought and sustained thought are the verbal formation; perception and feeling are the mental formation."

(Question) "Noble lady, why are in-breathing and out-breathing called the bodily formation? Why are applied thought and sustained thought called the verbal formation? Why are perception and feeling called the mental formation?"

(Answer) "Friend Visākha, in-breathing and out-breathing are bodily, these are bound up with the body (*ete dhammā kāya paṭibaddhā*); that is why in-breathing and out-breathing are called the bodily formation. Friend Visākha, first one applies thought and sustains thought, and then speaks words; that is why applied thought and sustained thought are called the verbal formation. Perception and feeling are mental, these are bound up with the mind (*ete dhammā citta paṭibaddhā*); that is why perception and feeling are called the mental formation."

MN 44 – The Shorter Series of Questions and Answers
(Cūḷavedalla Sutta)

One Who Sees Dependent Origination Sees the Dhamma

By understanding Dependent Origination, one understands the Noble Truth of suffering. By understanding the five aggregates of clinging, also, one understands the Noble Truth of suffering.

Once, the Venerable Sāriputta having explained how the five aggregates of clinging arise through the sense bases, further explained:

> He understands thus: "This, indeed, is how these five aggregates of clinging come together, gather together, exist as a whole. That is why the Blessed One said in this way: 'One who sees Dependent Origination sees the Dhamma; one who sees the Dhamma sees Dependent Origination.' And these five aggregates of clinging are dependently arisen. If there is desire, adoration, love, and zealous engagement toward these five aggregates of clinging, that is the origin of suffering. If desire and lust for these five aggregates of clinging are eliminated, if desire and lust are eradicated, that is the cessation of suffering." Venerable friends, just by that, that monk has accomplished much in the Buddha's Dispensation.
>
> MN 28 – The Greater Discourse on the Simile of the Elephant's Footprint (Mahāhatthipadopama Sutta)

The Attainment of Cessation

There is a state of meditative absorption where the meditator can experience the cessation of all three of the formations described in Dependent Origination—the bodily formation, the verbal formation, and the mental formation. It is called the attainment of cessation (*nirodha samāpatti*).

> **(Question)** "Noble lady, when a monk enters upon the attainment of the cessation of perception and feeling, what ceases first in him? The bodily formation? The verbal formation? Or the mental formation?"
>
> **(Answer)** "Friend Visākha, when a monk enters upon the attainment of the cessation of perception and feeling, first the verbal formation ceases, then the bodily formation, then the mental formation."
>
> MN 44 – The Shorter Series of Questions and Answers
> (Cūḷavedalla Sutta)

We can now understand through these definitions that the word "formations" (*saṅkhārā*) has several meanings. Not everyone can achieve the attainment of cessation (*nirodha samāpatti*) that we just discussed. One must first develop form and formless jhāna up to the level of neither-perception-nor-non-perception (*nevasaññānā-saññāyatana*). This is achieved through tranquility meditation (*samatha*). Next, insight (*vipassanā*) has to be developed to the level of a non-returner or to the level of an Arahant. Only such people can achieve the attainment of cessation (*nirodha samāpatti*). Hence, it is not mentioned in the Dhamma that an Arahant liberated by wisdom (*paññāvimutta*) who has developed concentration only up to the fourth jhāna is able to achieve the attainment of cessation.

As a result of misunderstanding this, some people have adopted the wrong view that Arahantship can be achieved through dry-insight meditation. According to their theory, right concentration (*sammā samādhi*) is not necessary to attain Arahantship. They talk about something called momentary concentration (*khaṇika samādhi*). However, in all the discourses where right concentration (*sammā samādhi*) is discussed, it is invariably the four jhānas that are described.

There are three components that make up the concentration aggregate of the Noble Eightfold Path—right effort, right mindfulness, and right concentration. When one rejects right concentration, all three of these factors of the path are rejected. Then the Noble Eightfold Path is reduced to five.

In this way, we can clearly understand the danger in the view that Arahantship can be achieved without jhānas.

Learn the Dhamma with Respect

Because the sacred Dhamma contains clear instructions, the first thing to do is to learn the Dhamma with respect and learn it well. One should not learn the Dhamma in order to promote one's own capricious theories. Those who pick up excerpts of the Dhamma on a whim and attempt to pompously pose as erudite Dhamma scholars spread falsehood instead of the Dhamma.

It is a pity that some take up the Mahāyāna Buddhist tradition, which is not a well-declared (*svākkhāta*) Dhamma. "Well-declared" means the teachings of the Blessed One, which are good in the beginning, good in the middle, good in the end, with the right meaning and phrasing (leading to the eradication of all defilements), which proclaim the perfectly complete and pure spiritual life. Mahāyāna Buddhism, on the other hand, is not well-declared, it is ill-declared (*durakkhāta*). Therefore, to take up Mahāyāna views in place of the Theravāda teachings is akin to seeking aluminum jewelry while already possessing gold jewelry.

The Venerable Sāriputta's Advice

Once, the Venerable Sāriputta gave some advice to a group of monks about to set out on a journey.

Have You Learned the Dhamma Well?

> Have you venerable ones heard and learned the Dhamma well? Are you well-versed in the Dhamma? Have you reflected well on the Dhamma? Have you thoroughly committed the Dhamma to memory? Have you realized the Dhamma with wisdom?

Essential Points to Consider

> Is it not so that when you teach the Dhamma you should: (1) State exactly what has been said by the Blessed One? (2) Should not misrepresent him with what is contrary to fact? (3) Should explain in accordance with the Dhamma, and (4) should not give rise to reasonable debate and criticism?
>
> SN 22.2 – At Devadaha (Devadaha Sutta)

Now we have studied Dependent Origination up to saṅkhārā. It is the Buddha who understood this principle of cause and effect. We, as his disciples, should be humble enough to learn the Dhamma in the exact manner that he taught it.

From What Do Formations Arise?

> When what exists do formations come to be? By what are formations conditioned? ... When there is ignorance,

formations come to be; formations have ignorance as their condition (*avijjā paccayā saṅkhārā*).

SN 12.10 – Gotama the Great Sakyan Sage (Gotama Sutta)

Chapter 16

Ignorance

The Buddha discovered that formations arise due to ignorance. Starting from that point, the Blessed One explained the complete process of Dependent Origination in this way: "With ignorance as condition, formations come to be. With formations as condition, consciousness comes to be. With consciousness as condition, name-and-form comes to be. With name-and-form as condition, the six sense bases come to be. With the six sense bases as condition, contact comes to be. With contact as condition, feeling comes to be. With feeling as condition, craving comes to be. With craving as condition, clinging comes to be. With clinging as condition, the arranging of kamma to bear fruit (*bhava*) comes to be. With the arranging of kamma to bear fruit as condition, birth (from an egg, from a womb, from moisture, and spontaneous birth) comes to be. With birth as condition, aging-and-death, sorrow, lamentation, pain, grief, and despair come to be."

"It is in this way that the whole mass of suffering comes to be (*evametassa kevalassa dukkhakkhandhassa samudayo hoti*)." Thus, Dependent Origination describes the process by which the suffering of beings in saṃsāra is created. Therefore, the ignorance which triggers this whole process should not be taken lightly.

What Is Ignorance?

> Monks, what is ignorance? Not realizing the noble truth of suffering, not realizing the noble truth of the origin of suffering, not realizing the noble truth of the cessation of suffering, not realizing the noble truth of the way leading to the cessation of suffering. This, monks, is called ignorance.
>
> SN 12.2 – Analysis of Dependent Origination (Vibhaṅga Sutta)

Ignorance Is Not Understanding the Four Noble Truths

Therefore, ignorance is having no understanding whatsoever of the Four Noble Truths. Because beings in saṃsāra dwell immersed in ignorance, there arise in them formations (*saṅkhārā*) due to ignorance. This means in-breathing and out-breathing occur affected by ignorance. Applied thought and sustained thought arise affected by ignorance. Perception and feeling arise affected by ignorance.

Therefore, as long as these formations affected by ignorance exist, consciousness of the eye, ear, nose, tongue, body, and mind arises based on ignorance. As a result, name (feeling, perception, volition, contact, and mental awareness) and form (the four great elements and things made up of the four great elements) arise based on ignorance. The six sense bases that are conditioned by name-and-form affected by ignorance invariably create an ignorance-based experience of the world.

Ignorance Must Be Eradicated to Eradicate Suffering

Monks, it is something like this. Suppose there is a building with a conical roof made by rafters joining a rounded wooden frame at the top. Thus, all of the rafters of this building are fastened to this rounded wooden frame at the top. If that wooden frame is broken, all those rafters would completely fall apart. Monks, in the same way, however many unwholesome roots there might be, all those unwholesome roots are based on ignorance, and lean against ignorance. Thus, if that ignorance were completely eradicated, all those unwholesome roots would also be eradicated.

SN 20.1 – The Roof Peak (Kūṭa Sutta)

The Most Powerful Hindrance

Monks, if there is a hindrance by which this generation of beings is enveloped, and therefore wanders in saṃsāra for ever so long—I see no other such hindrance, monks, as this hindrance of ignorance. Monks, this generation of beings enveloped by the hindrance known as ignorance (i.e., having no realization of the Four Noble Truths) runs on and wanders in saṃsāra for ever so long.

It – Ignorance (Avijjā Nīvaraṇa Sutta)

Lives Enveloped in Ignorance

It is indeed due to causes that our lives have fallen into the mass of suffering in saṃsāra, not without causes. As long as there are conditions that give rise to birth in saṃsāra, endless suffering and despair have to be experienced. When those conditions are destroyed, the formation of saṃsāra stops. Even regarding ignorance, what we should understand is not to search for the starting point of ignorance. We should instead understand why ignorance endures without being destroyed. If at this moment ignorance is within us, then the complete process of Dependent Origination is operating within us.

Looking for the Starting Point

> Monks, a starting point of ignorance cannot be shown, yet some say: "Before this there was no ignorance, it is something that came to be afterwards." Yet, it is clearly to be seen that ignorance is something that is conditioned.

Nutriment for Ignorance

> Monks, I say that ignorance, too, has a nutriment. I do not say that it is without nutriment. What is the nutriment for ignorance? It should be said: the five hindrances (*pañca nīvaraṇa*).
>
> AN 10.61 – Ignorance (Avijjā Sutta)

Dependent Origination Is the Wrong Path

The Buddha described Dependent Origination, which is based on ignorance, as the wrong path. A person's life guided by a wrong path is always in danger. It is not possible to gain true happiness, protection, or peace of mind by following a wrong path. Instead, the wrong path should be abandoned. In order to do this, it is necessary to understand how the wrong path—Dependent Origination—is formed and how it ceases. Only then it is possible to be liberated from it.

Chapter 17

Realization

> Monks, I will teach you about forty-four cases of gaining knowledge. Listen to that and attend closely, I will speak. Monks, what are the forty-four cases of gaining knowledge?
>
> (1) Knowledge of aging-and-death, (2) knowledge of the origin of aging-and-death, (3) knowledge of the cessation of aging-and-death, (4) knowledge of the way leading to the cessation of aging-and-death.
>
> SN 12.33 – Cases of Knowledge (1) (Ñāṇavatthu Sutta)

Similarly, it is necessary to understand each of the other factors of Dependent Origination in these same four ways: that is, (1) aging-and-death; (2) birth; (3) bhava; (4) clinging; (5) craving; (6) feeling; (7) contact; (8) the six sense bases; (9) name-and-form; (10) consciousness; (11) formations (in-breathing and out-breathing, applied thought and sustained thought, perception and feeling) should be understood in the four ways discussed above, yielding a forty-fourfold realization. This realization is called wisdom pertaining to the Dhamma (*dhamme ñāṇaṃ*). Through this realization, what one has gained is the realization of the Four Noble Truths.

This Is the Knowledge Pertaining to the Dhamma!

That is his knowledge pertaining to the Dhamma (*idamassa dhamme ñāṇaṃ*). By means of this Dhamma that he has seen and realized—that which is timeless, arrived at and oneself established in—he applies the same principle to the past and to the future (*so iminā dhammena diṭṭhena, viditena, akālikena, pattena, pariyogāḷhena, atītānāgatena nayaṃ neti*):

A Timeless Realization!

"If ascetics and brahmins in the past realized aging-and-death, realized the origin of aging-and-death, realized the cessation of aging-and-death, and realized the path leading to the cessation of aging-and-death, all of them realized in the very same way that I do now.

"If ascetics and brahmins in the future were to realize aging-and-death, realize the origin of aging-and-death, realize the cessation of aging-and-death, and realize the way leading to the cessation of aging-and-death, all of them will realize in the very same way that I do now." This is his knowledge gained by application according to the Dhamma (*idamassa anvaye ñāṇaṃ*).

Monks, if one day the noble disciple purely and clearly realizes these two kinds of knowledge—knowledge pertaining to the Dhamma (*dhamme ñāṇaṃ*) and knowledge gained by application according to the Dhamma (*anvaye ñāṇaṃ*)—monks, it is this noble disciple that is known as one who possesses right view, who possesses the vision of the Four Noble Truths, one who has arrived at this Dhamma, one who sees the Dhamma, the wise one who disciplines in the Noble Eightfold Path, one who has the knowledge of the Noble Eightfold Path, one who has entered the stream of the Dhamma, one who possesses the revulsion that makes one a noble person, one who stands squarely before the door to Nibbāna.

SN 12.33 – Cases of Knowledge (1) (Ñāṇavatthu Sutta)

One thing can be clearly understood from this discourse—that this is a truth that will not change over time. All the Buddhas of the past realized the same Dhamma. All the Buddhas of the future will realize the same Dhamma. That is the very Dhamma that was realized by Gotama Buddha, our teacher.

Do Not Divide into Time Periods

In some Buddhist books, Dependent Origination is not explained in the same way that it is explained in the sacred Dhamma. Later books, such as the *Visuddhimagga*, divide Dependent Origination into three time periods—past, present, and future. They mention five past causes, five present effects, five present causes, and five future effects. Yet, no such division is shown in any discourse by the Buddha. This is an exegesis that creates confusion after confusion and complicates the chance of understanding Dependent Origination. This can be considered non-Dhamma that has arisen as a result of attempts to analyze the Dhamma according to capricious methods. The following discourse will further clarify the matter.

Seventy-Seven Cases of Gaining Knowledge!

Monks, I will teach you seventy-seven cases of gaining knowledge ... Monks, what are the seventy-seven cases of gaining knowledge?

(1) The knowledge that aging-and-death has birth as its condition. (2) The knowledge that when there is no birth, there is no aging-and-death. (3) The knowledge that in the past aging-and-death had birth as its condition. (4) The knowledge that in the past too, when there was no birth, there was no aging-and-death. (5) The knowledge that in the future aging-and-death will have birth as its condition. (6) The knowledge that in the future too, when there is no birth, there will be no aging-and-death. (7) The knowledge that, if there is a realization regarding the existence of this law of Dependent Origination, that realization too, is subject to disintegration, subject to destruction, of such a nature that one should eradicate attachment toward it, of such a nature that one should cease attaching to it.

SN 12.34 – Cases of Knowledge (2) (Dutiya Ñāṇavatthu Sutta)

The Same Principle Applies to All Three Time Periods

In particular, a great deal of confusion has arisen due to the division of the contents of this discourse on Dependent Origination into time periods. The advocates of this approach have renamed consciousness as "rebirth-linking consciousness" (*paṭisandhicitta*). The term "rebirth-linking consciousness" does not appear in the original discourses of the Buddha at all. This division into three time periods only gives rise to a topic for debate and does not help in realizing the Dhamma.

It is possible to analyze and understand Dependent Origination through the *Dutiya Ñāṇavatthu Sutta,* in which the Blessed One showed how to understand Dependent Origination in the same manner in all three time periods.

The Same Principle Applies to the Past as Well

Now you can apply the same method to the rest of the factors of Dependent Origination. Then, it will be absolutely clear to you how unsuccessful is the exegetical device of dividing and explaining Dependent Origination by way of three time periods. According to how the Buddha explained it, in the past, too, birth was conditioned by the arranging of kamma to bear fruit. In the past, too, the arranging of kamma to bear fruit was conditioned by clinging. In the past, too, clinging was conditioned by craving. In the past, too, craving was conditioned by feeling. In the past, too, feeling was conditioned by contact. In the past, too, contact was conditioned by the six sense bases. In the past, too, the six sense bases were conditioned by name-and-form. In the past, too, name-and-form was conditioned by consciousness. In the past, too, consciousness was conditioned by formations. In the past, too, formations were conditioned by ignorance.

In the past, too, formations ceased with the cessation of ignorance. When you apply the law of Dependent Origination to the future in the same manner, then it is possible to better understand Dependent Origination.

Nine Great Insight Knowledges?

There is a series of knowledges described as the nine great insight knowledges, but we have not read about them in any of the original discourses of the Buddha. It is wise to investigate carefully before considering any teachings not found in the original discourses as the pure words of the Buddha. What interests us is the truth, not things that masquerade as the truth.

Recognizing the Dhamma

If a person says something, claiming it to be the word of the Buddha, the best thing to do is verify it against the original discourses of the Buddha.

If it can be verified against the word of the Buddha contained in the Suttas and the Vinaya, only then should it be accepted with great delight as the pure Dhamma of the Gotama Buddha.

Reject What Is Contrary to the Dhamma

If something quoted as Dhamma does not compare against the Suttas, and fails to agree with the Vinaya, then it should be rejected as something contrary to the Dhamma; it is falsehood in the guise of the pure Dhamma of the Buddha. Successfully identifying the Dhamma in this way can be accomplished only if one has a pure knowledge of the Dhamma taught by the Buddha.

The pure Dhamma is alive in the following sacred Dhamma collections: The Long Discourses of the Buddha (Dīgha Nikāya); The Middle-Length Discourses of the Buddha (Majjhima Nikāya); The Numerical Discourses of the

Buddha (Aṅguttara Nikāya); The Connected Discourses of the Buddha (Saṃyutta Nikāya); the Dhammapada; Inspired Utterances (Udāna); Itivuttaka; Sutta Nipāta; Verses of the Arahant Monks and Arahant Nuns (Theragāthā, Therīgāthā); Stories of Heavenly Mansions (Vimānavatthu); Stories of Ghosts (Petavatthu); Verses of Birth Stories (Jātaka). In addition, the pure Dhamma is found in the books of discipline (Vinaya Piṭaka)—Pārājikā Pāḷi, Pācittiya Pāḷi, Māhavagga Pāḷi, Cūllavagga Pāḷi, and Parivāra Pāḷi.

The Pure Dhamma!

We venerate the pure Dhamma saying *svākkhāto bhagavatā dhammo*. The word *svākkhāta* means well proclaimed. The only well-proclaimed Dhamma in this world is the Dhamma taught by the Buddha. It is for this reason that his Dhamma is described as *svākkhāta*. The beginning of this sacred Dhamma is excellent (*ādi kalyāṇaṃ*). It is excellent in the middle (*majjhe kalyāṇaṃ*), and excellent in the end (*pariyosāna kalyāṇaṃ*). The Dhamma is complete and pure in meaning (*sātthaṃ*). It is explained with very clear phrasing (*sabyañjanaṃ*). It proclaims the perfectly complete and pure spiritual life leading to Arahantship (*kevala paripuṇṇaṃ parisuddhaṃ brahmacariyaṃ abhivadati*).

Therefore, we should be fortunate to identify the pure Dhamma as the Dhamma. If not, in this life as well, we will lose this momentous opportunity to realize the sacred Dhamma.

Let Us Learn This by Heart

You should learn and memorize Dependent Origination in Pāli. Understand the meaning in detail. Then, gradually your skill in understanding will grow.

Dependent Origination in Pāli

Avijjā paccayā saṅkhārā
Saṅkhāra paccayā viññāṇaṃ
Viññāṇa paccayā nāmarūpaṃ
Nāmarūpa paccayā saḷāyatanaṃ
Saḷāyatana paccayā phasso
Phassa paccayā vedanā
Vedanā paccayā taṇhā
Taṇhā paccayā upādānaṃ
Upādāna paccayā bhavo
Bhava paccayā jāti
Jāti paccayā jarāmaraṇaṃ, soka, parideva, dukkha domanassupāyāsā sambhavanti.
Evametassa kevalassa dukkhakkhandhassa samudayo hoti.

Learn Dependent Origination in English as Well

With ignorance as condition, formations come to be; with formations as condition, consciousness comes to be; with consciousness as condition, name-and-form comes to be; with name-and-form as condition, the six sense bases come to be; with the six sense bases as condition, contact comes to be; with contact as condition, feeling comes to be; with feeling as condition, craving comes to be; with craving as condition, clinging comes to be; with clinging as condition, bhava comes to be; with bhava as condition, birth comes to be; with birth as condition, aging-and-death, sorrow, lamentation, pain, grief, and despair come to be. Such is the origin of this whole mass of suffering.

The moment the Buddha realized the law of Dependent Origination, he expressed his feelings in the following way:

> "Causally arising! Causally arising!"—thus, monks, in regard to the law of Dependent Origination unheard before there arose in me the eye of the Dhamma, knowledge, wisdom, true knowledge, and light.
>
> SN 12.10 – Gotama the Great Sakyan Sage (Gotama Sutta)

Dependent Origination Is Impermanent

Dependent Origination is conditioned by impermanent causes—there is nothing permanent to be found in Dependent Origination. The reason beings have fallen into this saṃsāra for such a long time is nothing but the continual formation of Dependent Origination.

The Lord of the Dhamma, the Buddha, described the law of Dependent Origination as the arising of suffering. Therefore, the cessation of suffering comes about when Dependent Origination does not exist. If effects arise from causes, it is natural for effects to cease when the causes are no more. Then, the Buddha investigated with wisdom how Dependent Origination ceases.

Chapter 18

Cessation

With the Cessation of Dependent Origination, Aging-and-Death Ceases!

> When what does not exist does aging-and-death not come to be? With the cessation of what does the cessation of aging-and-death come about?

The amazing wisdom of the Buddha was the only light capable of dispelling the pitch darkness in the world.

> When there is no birth, aging-and-death does not come to be; with the cessation of birth comes cessation of aging-and-death.

Because birth causes aging-and-death, birth has to cease for aging-and-death to cease.

The Cessation of Birth

> When what does not exist does birth not come to be? With the cessation of what does the cessation of birth come about?

This is truly the burning issue for the beings of the world, but they do not know it. When this problem is solved, all problems are solved.

When there is no bhava (i.e., the arranging of kamma to bear fruit—sense-sphere bhava, form-sphere bhava, and formless-sphere bhava), birth does not come to be; with the cessation of bhava comes the cessation of birth.

The Cessation of Bhava

Bhava (i.e., the arranging of kamma to bear fruit), too, is formed due to a cause. Therefore, for bhava to cease the cause has to cease.

When what does not exist does bhava not come to be? With the cessation of what, does the cessation of bhava come about?

When there is no clinging (clinging to sensual pleasures, clinging to views, clinging to behaviors and observances, and clinging to a notion of self) bhava does not come to be; with the cessation of clinging, comes the cessation of bhava.

The Cessation of Clinging

Clinging is also dependently arisen and subject to cessation when the necessary cause is absent.

When what does not exist, does clinging not come to be? With the cessation of what, does the cessation of clinging come about?

When there is no craving (i.e., craving for forms, craving for sounds, craving for odors, craving for flavors, craving for tangibles, and craving for mental phenomena) clinging does not come to be; with the cessation of craving, comes the cessation of clinging.

The Cessation of Craving

When what does not exist, does craving not come to be? With the cessation of what, does the cessation of craving come about?

When there is no feeling (i.e., feeling born of eye-contact, feeling born of ear-contact, feeling born of nose-contact, feeling born of tongue-contact, feeling born of body-contact, and feeling born of mind-contact) craving does not come to be; with the cessation of feeling, comes the cessation of craving.

The Cessation of Feeling

When what does not exist, does feeling not come to be? With the cessation of what, does the cessation of feeling come about?

When there is no contact (i.e., eye-contact, ear-contact, nose-contact, tongue-contact, body-contact, and mind-contact) feeling does not come to be; with the cessation of contact, comes the cessation of feeling.

The Cessation of Contact

When what does not exist, does contact not come to be? With the cessation of what, does the cessation of contact come about?

When there are no six sense bases (i.e., the eye base, the ear base, the nose base, the tongue base, the body base, and the mind base) contact does not come to be; with the cessation of the six sense bases, comes the cessation of contact.

The Cessation of the Six Sense Bases

When what does not exist, do the six sense bases not come to be? With the cessation of what, does the cessation of the six sense bases come about?

When there is no name-and-form (name consisting of feeling, perception, volition, contact, and mental awareness, and form consisting of the four great elements and all things made up of the four great elements) the six sense bases do not come to be; with the cessation of name-and-form, comes the cessation of the six sense bases.

The Cessation of Name-and-Form

When what does not exist, does name-and-form not come to be? With the cessation of what, does the cessation of name-and-form come about?

When there is no consciousness (i.e., eye-consciousness, ear-consciousness, nose-consciousness, tongue-consciousness, body-consciousness, and mind-consciousness) name-and-form does not come to be; with the cessation of consciousness, comes the cessation of name-and-form.

The Cessation of Consciousness

When what does not exist, does consciousness not come to be? With the cessation of what, does the cessation of consciousness come about?

When there are no formations (the bodily formation, in-breathing and out-breathing; the verbal formation, applied thought and sustained thought; and the mental formation, perception and feeling) consciousness does not come to be; with the cessation of formations, comes the cessation of consciousness.

The Cessation of Formations

When what does not exist, do formations not come to be? With the cessation of what, does the cessation of formations come about?

When there is no ignorance (having no realization of the Four Noble Truths), formations do not come to be; with the cessation of ignorance, comes the cessation of formations.

Ignorance Also Ceases!

Ignorance ceases when full realization of the Four Noble Truths is attained. Realizing the Four Noble Truths is the arising of true knowledge (*vijjā*) and the eradication of ignorance. Where there is true knowledge, there is no craving, and freedom from craving is liberation. The attainment of true knowledge and liberation is freedom from all suffering.

Then Dependent Origination ceases permanently. All suffering and despair are ended forever. The cessation of Dependent Origination is called the right path.

Let Us Learn by Heart the Right Path, the Cessation of Dependent Origination

With the complete disappearance and cessation of ignorance comes cessation of formations; with the cessation of formations, comes cessation of consciousness; with the cessation of consciousness, comes cessation of name-and-form; with the cessation of name-and-form, comes cessation of the six sense bases; with the cessation of the six sense bases, comes cessation of contact; with the cessation of contact, comes cessation of feeling; with the cessation of feeling, comes cessation of craving; with the cessation of craving, comes cessation of clinging; with the cessation of clinging, comes cessation of bhava; with the cessation of bhava, comes cessation of birth; with the cessation of birth, aging-and-death, sorrow, lamentation, pain, grief, and despair cease. Such is the cessation of this whole mass of suffering.

Let Us Learn the Cessation of Dependent Origination in Pāli

Avijjāyat'veva asesa virāga nirodhā saṅkhāra nirodho;
saṅkhāranirodhā viññāṇa nirodho;
viññāṇa nirodhā nāmarūpa nirodho;
nāmarūpa nirodhā saḷāyatana nirodho;
saḷāyatana nirodhā phassa nirodho;
phassa nirodhā vedanā nirodho;
vedanā nirodhā taṇhā nirodho;
taṇhā nirodhā upādāna nirodho;
upādāna nirodhā bhava nirodho;
bhava nirodhā jāti nirodho;
jāti nirodhā jarāmaraṇaṃ soka, parideva, dukkha, domanassupāyāsā nirujjhanti.
Evametassa kevalassa dukkhakkhandhassa nirodho hoti.

"With the cessation of causes comes cessation! With the cessation of causes, cessation!"—thus, monks, in regard to the law of Dependent Origination unheard before there arose in me the eye of the Dhamma, knowledge, wisdom, true knowledge, and light.

SN 12.10 – Gotama the Great Sakyan Sage (Gotama Sutta)

Chapter 19

Essential Points to Keep in Mind

We, as disciples of the Buddha, should learn his Dhamma with much respect and seek refuge in that Dhamma itself. Thus, we should embrace the leadership of the Dhamma and Vinaya; no one else in the world has such a pure, supreme, honorable leadership. The leadership of the Dhamma and Vinaya is unsurpassed.

Yet, if a monk or a lay-disciple claims, "Oh! Buddhists do not have a leader!" that person would indeed be one who does not know Dhamma-Vinaya. What we in fact are lacking is not Buddhist leadership but Buddhist discipleship. A Buddhist disciple is one who accepts the leadership of the Dhamma and the Vinaya.

The Noble Law

The Blessed One described the correct method of understanding Dependent Origination as the "noble law." This method is described in the following manner in the Pañcabhayavera Sutta of the Saṃyutta Nikāya:

> Here, householder, it is on Dependent Origination itself that the noble disciple in the Buddha's Dispensation contemplates with wisdom thus: "When this exists, that

comes to be (*imasmiṃ sati idaṃ hoti*); with the arising of this, that arises (*imassa uppādā idaṃ uppajjati*)."

SN 12.41 – Five Fearful Animosities (Pañcabhayavera Sutta)

Now, in the above formula for Dependent Origination, replace the word "this" with ignorance. Then, replace the word "that" with formations. Then you have: "When ignorance exists, formations come to be. With the arising of ignorance, formations arise."

You can apply this method to all the links of Dependent Origination.

The Law of the Origin of Suffering

When ignorance exists, formations come to be. With the arising of ignorance, formations arise.

When formations exist, consciousness come to be. With the arising of formations, consciousness arises.

When consciousness exists…

The Law of the Cessation of Suffering

The Blessed One also showed us a method of understanding the cessation of suffering:

When this does not exist, that does not come to be (*imasmiṃ asati idaṃ na hoti*); with the cessation of this, that ceases (*imassa nirodhā idaṃ nirujjhati*).

Just as in the above example, we can relate this formula to Dependent Origination:

When ignorance does not exist, formations do not come to be; with the cessation of ignorance, formations cease.

> When formations do not exist, consciousness does not come to be; with the cessation of formations, consciousness ceases.
>
> When consciousness does not exist...
>
> When bhava does not exist, birth does not come to be; with the cessation of bhava, birth ceases.
>
> When birth does not exist, aging-and-death does not come to be; with the cessation of birth, aging-and-death ceases.
>
> SN 12.41 – Five Fearful Animosities (1)
> (Pañcabhayavera Sutta)

Right view is the starting point in understanding this Dhamma. A very clear understanding of cause and effect is necessary in order to develop right view. In particular, wise consideration is extremely helpful in this regard. Even for developing serenity and insight meditation, it is wise consideration that is essential. The sacred Dhamma is not something that can be understood without commitment.

What Is Direct Realization?

Direct realization is not subject to change. When a person's arm or leg is amputated, he or she definitely knows that the arm or leg does not exist. It is impossible for an amputated limb to grow back.

Similarly, if something is directly realized, it is impossible to lose that understanding over time. It will not happen under any circumstances. However, without knowing what direct realization is, some people arrive at the conclusion that they possess a direct realization based on trivial experiences. But as time passes, their understanding becomes just a memory, as if experienced in a dream. Then that person thinks direct realization is something that deteriorates, but the reality is quite different: that person was in fact deluded into having a direct realization without actually possessing such.

Direct Realization Should Go beyond the Following

Once, the Venerable Saviṭṭha, the Venerable Mūsila, the Venerable Nārada, and the Venerable Ānanda were dwelling at Kosambī in Ghosita's Park. Then, the Venerable Saviṭṭha asked the Venerable Mūsila:

> Venerable friend Mūsila, apart from mere confidence, apart from personal preference, apart from hearsay, apart from reasoned reflection, apart from taking up a view, does the Venerable Mūsila have a realization gained by oneself thus: "With birth as condition, aging-and-death comes to be?"

The Venerable Mūsila replied in this way:

> Venerable friend Saviṭṭha, apart from mere confidence, apart from personal preference, apart from hearsay, apart from reasoned reflection, apart from taking up a view, I know this, I see this: "With birth as condition, aging-and-death comes to be."

SN 12.68 – Kosambī (Kosambiya Sutta)

When the Venerable Saviṭṭha questioned the Venerable Mūsila in this way about how Dependent Origination arises and ceases, all the questions were answered in a similar manner. Then, the Venerable Saviṭṭha asked the Venerable Mūsila: "So, venerable friend Mūsila, you are an Arahant, aren't you?" When he was asked thus, the Venerable Mūsila remained silent. Venerable Mūsila was truly a liberated monk (Arahant).

Before achieving direct realization, according to the Buddha, knowledge can only be gained in the five ways shown below:

(1). Knowledge based on confidence (*saddhā*)

(2). Knowledge based on personal preference (*ruci*)

(3). Knowledge based on hearsay (*anussava*)

(4). Knowledge based on reasoned reflection (*ākāra parivitakka*)

(5). Knowledge based on taking up a view (*diṭṭhinijjānakkhanti*)

Direct realization goes beyond these five bases for knowledge. It is doubtful whether such a modern and rational method of explaining direct realization could be found in the present-day world. Through this alone, an intelligent person can appreciate how modern and rational is the understanding of the Buddha.

The Direct Realization of the Arahant

It is now clear to us that direct realization is something that goes beyond the five methods of gaining knowledge explained above. One who has achieved the cessation of Dependent Origination has achieved Nibbāna as well. The attainment of Nibbāna is experiential. This is explained in the following discourse:

> Venerable friend Mūsila, apart from mere confidence, apart from personal preference, apart from hearsay, apart from reasoned reflection, apart from taking up a view, does the Venerable Mūsila have a realization gained by oneself thus: "Nibbāna is the cessation of bhava?"
>
> SN 12.68 – Kosambī (Kosambiya Sutta)

The Venerable Mūsila replied that he had achieved the direct realization that Nibbāna is the cessation of bhava.

Not All Arahants Possess Psychic Powers

Possessing psychic powers does not necessary mean that a person is an Arahant. A person does not become an Arahant by gaining psychic powers; a person becomes an Arahant by gaining the knowledge of the destruction of the taints (*āsavakkhaya ñāṇa*). Not all Arahants possess psychic powers, but all Arahants have fully developed the Noble Eightfold Path.

They have achieved complete realization of the Dhamma taught by the Buddha and have attained the highest bliss of Nibbāna. Arahants are the disciples who have arrived at the essence of the Buddha's Dispensation.

The Distinction Between the Buddha and an Arahant Disciple

The Buddha was the first human being to attain Enlightenment without the guidance of a teacher. His disciples attained Enlightenment with the help of the Buddha's guidance. Once, the Buddha questioned his disciples on this in the following manner:

Monks, the Tathāgata, the Arahant, the Perfectly Self-Enlightened One, having experienced revulsion toward form, having eradicated attachment toward it, having eliminated attachment toward it—thus unattached to form and liberated from it—is therefore called a Perfectly Self-Enlightened One. Monks, in the same way, a monk, having experienced revulsion toward form, having eradicated attachment toward it, having eliminated attachment toward it—thus unattached to form and liberated from it—is therefore called one liberated by wisdom (*paññāvimutta*).

Monks, the Tathāgata, the Arahant, the Perfectly Self-Enlightened One, having experienced revulsion toward feeling ... perception ... volitional formations ... consciousness, having eradicated attachment toward it, having eliminated attachment toward it—thus unattached to consciousness and liberated from it—is therefore called a Perfectly Self-Enlightened One. Monks, in the same way, a monk, having experienced revulsion toward feeling ... perception ... volitional formations ... consciousness, having eradicated attachment toward it, having eliminated attachment toward it—thus unattached to consciousness and liberated from it—is therefore called one liberated by wisdom.

Monks, therein what is the distinction, what is meant by this, what is the difference between the Tathāgata, the Arahant, the Perfectly Self-Enlightened One, and a monk liberated by wisdom?

Then the monks replied thus:

Venerable sir, our Dhamma is indeed based in the Blessed One, has the Blessed One as the foremost authority, takes recourse in the Blessed One. Venerable sir, it would be good if the Blessed One himself would shed light on the meaning of this statement. It is what is heard from the Blessed One that the monks retain in mind.

The Distinction

Then, the Blessed One explained the difference between himself and the Arahant in the following manner:

Monks, the Tathāgata, the Arahant, the Perfectly Self-Enlightened One, is the originator of the path to Nibbāna unoriginated before, the one who gives rise to the path to Nibbāna unarisen before, the declarer of the path to Nibbāna undeclared before [by anyone among devas and humans, Māra, and Brahmas, ascetics and brahmins]. He is the knower of the path to Nibbāna, the revealer of the path to Nibbāna, the one highly skilled in the path to Nibbāna. And monks, his disciples now dwell tracing his footsteps along that path to Nibbāna.

Monks, this is the distinction, the meaning, the difference between the Tathāgata, the Arahant, the Perfectly Self-Enlightened One, and a monk liberated by wisdom.

SN 22.58 – The Perfectly Enlightened One
(Sambuddha Sutta)

Foremost in the World

> To whatever extent, monks, there are abodes of beings, even up to the pinnacle of existence, these are the foremost in the world, these are the greatest, that is, the Arahants.
>
> SN 22.76 – Arahants (1) (Paṭhama Arahanta Sutta)

Free from Dependent Origination

The Arahant is a person of the highest caliber, one who is free from Dependent Origination. For the Arahant who has extirpated ignorance, freed himself from craving, and attained the knowledge of the destruction of the taints, how could there ever arise Dependent Origination born of ignorance? It could never happen.

The Mind Freed

On one occasion, the Venerable Arahant Soṇa explained the nature of the Arahant's mind in the presence of the Buddha:

> Venerable sir, when a monk is thus perfectly liberated in mind, even if numerous forms cognizable by the eye come into range of the eye, they do not overwhelm his mind; his mind is not at all affected by the forms. It remains steady, imperturbable, and he observes the impermanence of them all. Even if numerous sounds cognizable by the ear come into range of the ear … Even if numerous odors cognizable by the nose come into range of the nose … Even if numerous flavors cognizable by the tongue come into range of the tongue … Even if numerous tangibles cognizable by the body

> come into range of the body ... Even if numerous mental phenomena cognizable by the mind come into range of the mind, they do not overwhelm his mind; his mind is not at all affected by the mental phenomena. It remains steady, imperturbable, and he observes the impermanence of them all.
>
> Suppose, venerable sir, there were a rocky mountain, without clefts or fissures, one solid mass. If a violent rainstorm should come from the east, it could not make it quake, wobble, and tremble; if a violent rainstorm should come from the west ... from the north ... from the south, it could not make it quake, wobble, and tremble.
>
> AN 6.55 – Soṇa (Soṇa Sutta)

Do Not Go Astray

There are many in the world who turn the discourses of the Buddha inside out and misinterpret their meaning. They do not wish to talk about the Dhamma as the Dhamma. Adopting various views born of unwise consideration and seeking for evidence to support their arguments are commonplace.

As a result, they ignore even the points that are clearly explained in the original discourses. Instead, they put forth various other views and arguments. There is an account in the Saṃyutta Nikāya about a monk named Susīma who realized the Dhamma after listening to the Buddha teach on Dependent Origination. We find certain misinterpretations of that discourse claiming that it is about a monk who attained Arahantship through dry-insight meditation without attaining the jhānas. Therefore, it is useful for all of us to properly learn the points contained in that discourse.

The Story of Susīma

Susīma, an ascetic belonging to another religious sect, was entrusted with a serious responsibility by his sect. He was instructed to obtain ordination from the Buddha and learn the Dhamma while mingling with the monks. The intent was to return to his sect with the knowledge of the Dhamma acquired in this way and teach the Dhamma as if it were their own to win over the hearts of the people. Having accepted the serious responsibility of carrying out this devious scheme, Susīma came to the Venerable Ānanda and requested ordination. The Venerable Ānanda, with the Buddha's permission, ordained Susīma.

From the day he was ordained, the monk Susīma was out to steal the Dhamma Therefore, he was more eager than others to learn the Dhamma. Nevertheless, for the monk Susīma, who remained ever inquisitive about the lives of the monks, there arose a serious question in his mind.

Many monks would come to the Buddha and declare the attainment of Arahantship, but they did not display any psychic powers: they did not speak of having obtained the divine eye; they did not declare that they were able read the minds of others; they did not speak about having the ability to recollect their past lives; they did not speak about possessing the knowledge of the passing away and reappearance of beings; those Arahants did not mention that they were able to touch with their bodies and dwell in those peaceful, formless states that transcend form jhānas. However, they would still declare themselves to be Arahants.

Bewildered

The monk Susīma was confounded by this situation. What fazed him the most was the disparity between what he was seeing and hearing and his conception of an Arahant. Susīma approached monks who declared Arahantship and asked them whether they had attained certain higher knowledges (*abhiññā*). They replied that they had not attained such supernormal knowledges. Then, Susīma asked how they had become Arahants. "Venerable friend Susīma, we have been liberated by wisdom," they replied.

Arahants are divided into two primary types, those liberated in both respects (*ubhatobhāgavimutta*) and those liberated by wisdom (*paññāvimutta*). Arahants liberated in both respects have transcended the form jhānas, developed the formless jhānas up to the sphere of neither-perception-nor-non-perception, and thereby attained Arahantship.

Arahants liberated by wisdom are those who have attained the culmination of right concentration (*sammā samādhi*) by developing the four form jhānas and thereby attained Arahantship.

The Buddha Guides Susīma

Finally, the monk Susīma decided to ask the Buddha and find the answers to his questions from him instead of asking anyone else. He went to see the Blessed One and told him of all the conversations he had had with the monks. Then, the Buddha explained to him how realization of the Dhamma dawns upon a disciple.

This Is Realization

> First, Susīma, comes knowledge of the stability in the Dhamma (*dhammaṭṭhiti ñāṇaṃ*), afterwards knowledge of Nibbāna.
>
> SN 12.70 – Susīma (Susīma Sutta)

The monk Susīma asked the Buddha to explain in detail what had been stated in brief. By then he no longer had the intention of stealing the Dhamma, rather, he was focused on finding the solution to his problem. Knowing this, the Blessed One explained the true nature of the five aggregates of clinging and the arising and cessation of the law of Dependent Origination.

The Monk Susīma Achieves Realization

At the end of the discourse, the unexpected happened: Susīma who had come to steal the Dhamma actually realized the Dhamma. But he himself did not attain any of the higher knowledges or formless jhānas he had come to expect of an Arahant. Based on this alone, it cannot reasonably be inferred that the Venerable Susīma became an Arahant through dry-insight without the form jhānas.

The Buddha questioned the Venerable Susīma in the same manner in which Susīma had questioned the monks who declared Arahantship before. Then, the Venerable Susīma prostrated himself at the feet of the Blessed One—he revealed his devious scheme to steal the Dhamma and asked for forgiveness.

The Venerable Susīma Was Also Liberated by Wisdom

With regard to the transformation in the Venerable Susīma's life, many people think that he became an Arahant through dry-insight. The reason for this misconception is to be found in the following dialog:

> "Then knowing and seeing thus, Susīma, do you dwell in those peaceful deliverances that transcend form jhānas, the formless attainments, having touched them with the body?"
>
> "No, venerable sir."

There Are No Arahants Without Jhānas

It cannot be inferred in any way whatsoever from the above dialog that the Venerable Susīma had not attained any jhānas. No one can become an Arahant without fulfilling virtue, concentration, and wisdom. Accordingly, a clear understanding of Dependent Origination is very helpful for developing wisdom. This is what is referred to in the Dhamma as knowledge of the stability of the Dhamma, the law of the Dhamma, specific conditionality, Dependent Origination (*dhammaṭṭhiti dhammaniyāmatā. Idappaccayatā paṭiccasamuppādo*).

The Wheel of Dependent Origination?

In many modern books, Dependent Origination is explained by way of a symbolic wheel or circle. More than conveying the idea that any point on the wheel can be understood by contemplating in either direction (clockwise or anti-clockwise), what is actually described is the division of Dependent Origination into three time periods.

The Dispensation Will Disappear

Some people try to understand Dependent Origination by putting its twelve factors into a wheel. However, we did not come across a wheel when we studied Dependent Origination through the sacred word of the Buddha contained in his discourses. It is not possible to understand Dependent Origination by drawing circles, sketches, and diagrams. Therefore, Dependent Origination is not something to be drawn inside circles or wheels, rather it should be understood as a noble law.

In the present-day, it is more difficult to explain the original teachings of the Buddha to Buddhists than non-Buddhists. This is due to various corrupted views being spread within Buddhist society in the name of the pure Dhamma. As a result, instead of making an effort to learn the pure Dhamma, many people degrade and demean the pure Dhamma by constructing various views that are contrary to the pure Dhamma. In some cases, even monks are engaged in propagating these wrong views.

Personal views and opinions do not constitute the Buddha's Dispensation. The Buddha's instructions are the Buddha's Dispensation. What we have learned about Dependent Origination is the Buddha's Dispensation.

The Value of Right View

> Monks, in this way, of such great benefit is realizing the Dhamma, of such great benefit is obtaining the vision of the Dhamma.
>
> SN 13.1 – The Fingernail (Nakhasikhā Sutta)

So too, monks, the realization gained by ascetics, brahmins, and wanderers of other sects does not amount to a hundredth part, or a thousandth part, or a hundred thousandth part of the realization gained by a noble disciple who has realized the Four Noble Truths, a person possessing right view (i.e., a stream-enterer).

Monks, in this way, a person accomplished in right view possesses great realization and excellent wisdom.

SN 13.11 – The Mountain (3) (Tatiya Pabbatūpama Sutta)

For the Buddha's Dispensation to Exist for a Long Time...

Monks, there are these two things that lead to the destruction and disappearance of the Dhamma (the Buddha's Dispensation). What two?

(1). Badly set down words and phrases

(2). Wrong interpretation of the meaning

Monks, when the words and phrases are badly set down, then surely the meaning is wrongly interpreted. Monks, these are the two things that lead to the destruction and disappearance of the Dhamma (the Buddha's Dispensation).

Monks, there are these two things that lead to the continuation, non-destruction, and non-disappearance of the Dhamma. What two? Well set down words and phrases and the right interpretation of the meaning. Monks, when the words and phrases are well set down, then surely the meaning is interpreted rightly. Monks, these are the two things that lead to the continuation, non-destruction, and non-disappearance of the Dhamma (the Buddha's Dispensation).

AN 2.20 – Disciplinary Issues (Adhikaraṇa Vagga)

Beware

Monks, one who encourages another in a wrongly expounded Dhamma and discipline, and the one whom he encourages, and the one who, thus encouraged, practices in accordance with it, all accrue much demerit. What is the reason for that? Because that Dhamma is wrongly expounded.

AN 1.320 – One Thing (Ekadhammapāḷi Vagga)

Monks, those monks who explain Dhamma as non-Dhamma ... non-discipline as discipline ... discipline as non-discipline ... what has not been stated and uttered by the Tathāgata as having been stated and uttered by him ... what has been stated and uttered by the Tathāgata as not having been stated and uttered by him ... what has not been practiced by the Tathāgata as having been practiced by him ... what has been practiced by the Tathāgata as not having been practiced by him ... what has not been decreed by the Tathāgata as having been decreed by him ... what has been decreed by the Tathāgata as not having been decreed by him are acting for the harm of many people, for the ill of many people, for the ruin, harm, and suffering of many people, of devas and humans. Monks, those monks accrue much demerit and they are the ones who cause this Dhamma (the Buddha's Dispensation) to disappear.

AN 1.131-139 – Internal (Ajjhattika Vagga)

For the Protection of the Dispensation

Monks, those monks who explain Dhamma as Dhamma ... non-discipline as non-discipline ... discipline as discipline ... what has not been stated and uttered by the Tathāgata as not having been stated and uttered by him ... what has been stated and uttered by the Tathāgata as having been stated and uttered by him ... what has not been practiced by the Tathāgata as not having been practiced by him ... what has been practiced by the Tathāgata as having been practiced by him ... what has not been decreed by the Tathāgata as not having been decreed by him ... what has been decreed by the Tathāgata as having been decreed by him are acting for the welfare of many people, for the happiness of many people, for the good, welfare, and happiness of many people, of devas and humans. Monks, those monks accrue much merit and they are the ones who act for the continuance of this Dhamma (the Buddha's Dispensation).

AN 1.141-149 – Non-Dhamma (Adhamma Vagga)

Let Us Eradicate Poverty

Insignificant, monks, is the loss of wealth. The worst thing to lose is wisdom.

Insignificant, monks, is the gain of wealth. Monks, of all gains, the gain of wisdom is foremost. Therefore, monks, you should train yourselves thus: "We will develop in wisdom." Monks, it is in such a way that you should train yourselves.

AN 1.78-79 – Good Friendship (Kalyāṇamitta Vagga)

A Rare Opportunity

> Monks, in this Jambudīpa, delightful parks, groves, landscapes, and ponds are few, yet more numerous are the cliffs and slopes, rivers and caverns, ditches, places with thorns, and rugged mountains. In the same way, those beings are few who get to hear the Dhamma and Discipline expounded by the Tathāgata; more numerous are those who do not get to hear the Dhamma and Discipline expounded by the Tathāgata.
>
> AN 1.339 – One Thing (Ekadhammapāḷi Vagga)

What You Must Accomplish

Learn the teachings of the Buddha with great love and respect. Discuss the Dhamma with confidence (*saddhā*). Avoid getting caught up in reckless views. Listen to the pure Dhamma as it is, retain it in mind, and then direct your wisdom for the purpose of realization.

Have compassion on people, both Buddhists and non-Buddhists who are unaware of the pure Dhamma. Teach this Dhamma to them and bring comfort to their lives.

Teach this sacred Dhamma to your husband, wife, children, brothers and sisters, friends, relatives, and everyone you know and love. Compassionately help them understand the distinction between Dhamma and non-Dhamma. If you can think wisely, do not squander this rare, opportune human life; strive earnestly to become at least a stream-enterer in this very life.

If you are young and desire to ordain in this rare Dispensation of the Buddha, to learn the sacred Dhamma well, to practice and train in it, and to spread the Dhamma around the globe—dedicate your life to this purpose. Make it your life's sole purpose to learn, realize, and spread the Dhamma.

Protect Yourself, Protect the Dispensation

Your confidence will protect you. Confidence in the Triple Gem—Buddha, Dhamma, and the Noble Saṅgha, the community of disciples who attained stages of Enlightenment—is your protection. Without confidence in the Triple Gem, one lacks protection. One lacking confidence sees no value in the Triple Gem and finds fault with the Triple Gem for personal reasons, disparaging and forsaking the Triple Gem. Thereafter, it is impossible to prevent such a person from seeking refuge in beliefs based on wrong view.

However, if you possess firm confidence in the Triple Gem, you will not give it up even for the sake of your life. Your confidence will rescue you from wrong views. Established in confidence, you will gradually gain ingress into the sacred Dhamma and seek comfort only in the Dhamma. By following the Noble Eightfold Path, you will become a noble citizen of the world who possesses qualities of integrity, one who acts for the well-being of himself and others. Then you will live by the Dhamma and share it with others. Hence, if you were to decline in the Dhamma, it would also signify the decline of the Dhamma. On the other hand, if you establish yourself in the Dhamma, the Dhamma and the Dispensation will flourish.

This Is the Last Moment

You can make this moment the most precious moment of your life through the Dhamma. Devote at least a bit of time in life to spreading the noble Dhamma—the greatest treasure of wisdom bestowed upon humanity. You should definitely commit some time to that noble endeavor! Direct your Dhamma service for the lasting protection of the human race!

This book contains only a drop of water taken from the vast ocean that is the marvelous realization of the Buddha. May the merit acquired by writing this book help both you and I to realize the noble Dhamma rich with the taste of liberation, and to attain as soon as possible the supreme bliss of Nibbāna!

Namo tassa bhagavato arahato sammāsambuddhassa!

Homage to the Blessed One, the Arahant, the
Perfectly Self-Enlightened One!

Bibliography

I. Pāli Texts

Buddha Jayanti Tripiṭaka Series, Sinhala-script

II. Sutta Piṭaka Translations

Bhikkhu, Ven. Kiribathgoda Ñāṇānanda, Sinhala trans. 2014. Mahamevnawa Bodhiñāṇa Tripiṭaka Series. Polgahawela: Mahamegha Publishers.

Bodhi, Bhikkhu, trans. 2000. Connected Discourses of the Buddha: A Translation of the Saṃyutta Nikāya. Boston: Wisdom Publications.

———, trans. 2012. Numerical Discourses of the Buddha: A Translation of the Aṅguttara Nikāya. Boston: Wisdom Publications.

———, trans. 2017. The Suttanipāta: An Ancient Collection of the Buddha's Discourses Together with Its Commentaries. Boston: Wisdom Publications.

———, Bodhi, Bhikkhu, trans. 1995. The Great Discourse on Causation: The Mahānidāna Sutta and Its Commentaries. 2nd edition. Kandy: Buddhist Publication Society.

Ireland, John D., trans. 1997. The Udāna and the Itivuttka: Two Classics from the Pali Canon. Kandy: Buddhist Publication Society.

Ñāṇamoli, Bhikkhu, trans. 2009. The Middle Length Discourses of the Buddha: A Translation of the Majjhima Nikāya. Ed. and rev. by Bhikkhu Bodhi. 4th edition. Boston: Wisdom Publications.